Being Magickal

Spell's, Potion's, Empowerment, & More

More

For pre-teen to adult

Written By Lori Wayfair

Dedication

To the Divine Spirit and Yeshua, my Savior: For Your unwavering faithfulness and boundless goodness, guiding my path and illuminating my journey. Your presence is the cornerstone of my existence.

To the Holy Angels and Unseen Guardians: For your constant vigilance and ethereal support, whispering wisdom in moments of doubt, and weaving miracles into the fabric of my days. Your celestial influence has been my unseen strength.

To the Metaphysical Helpers and Spiritual Guides: For bridging the seen and unseen realms, opening doors to higher consciousness, and helping me navigate the intricate tapestry of existence. Your subtle energies have shaped my spiritual journey.

To Mila, my miracle daughter: Your brilliance at just nine years old inspires me daily. You are the light that brightens my world, a testament to the magick that flows through our bloodline. Your innate wisdom reminds me of the mysteries yet to unfold.

To Jonah, my steadfast husband: Your unwavering support has been my foundation. Thank you for believing in me and standing by my side through every chapter of our story, both in this physical realm and beyond.

This book is a testament to the love, faith, and support that have shaped my life and made this work possible. It is an offering to the seen and unseen forces that dance eternally in the cosmic ballet of creation.

About the Author

Lori Wayfair is an author, adventurer, and Priestess of Light with a rich and diverse background that has shaped her unique perspective on life. Born in Northern Michigan and raised in the United States, Lori has lived in an impressive 28 out of the 50 states, and her travels have taken her to all but 5 States. Lori has explored 6 countries, adding an international flavor to her experiences.

Married to her native German Husband, Jonah and blessed with a daughter, Lori has embraced the role of a dedicated wife and mother. A strong advocate for homeschooling, she actively engages in her daughter's education, fostering a love for learning and a deep connection to the world around them.

Lori's homestead is a lively haven filled with a menagerie of animals. From chickens and rabbits to a beagle dog and two cats, her farm is a bustling hub of activity.

Lori is a Priestess of Light. Her spiritual journey has taken her through numerous trials and moments of growth, shaping her into the resilient and enlightened individual she is today. Her connection to spirituality is deeply woven into the fabric of her life, influencing her perspectives and actions.

Nature holds a special place in Lori's heart, and she often finds solace and inspiration in the great outdoors. Her passion for writing is evident in her work, where she shares her insights on life, spirituality, and the joys of family.

Lori's life is a tapestry of diverse experiences, and her journey continues to unfold with each passing day. Lori embodies a multifaceted woman with a deep appreciation for the beauty and richness of life.

Table of Contents

<u>Prologue</u>

"Seek not to understand that you may believe,

but believe that you may understand."

-Saint Augustine

Most of us are born with a sense of wonderment for life and an awareness of Magick.

Often, events, religion, politics, science, peers, family, confusion, wrong doings, exhaustion, sickness, and heart break can water down our conscious self and our natural connection with Magick.

This book offers direct ways to connect with Magick and its Source. Enabling you to connect more deeply to yourself which in return will aid you to create a more rewarding relationship with Magick and the Divine.

I implore you, reader, to not take Magick or the contents in this book lightly. For every action there is a reaction. All the energy we send out comes back to us in one way or another.

Also don't take things too seriously and have fun being creative with the wonder of Magick. A childlike heart goes a long way.

I suggest keeping a journal or several journals to record and review practices and experiences.

I am excited for you as you start or further your Magickal journey.

Be blessed and kept in Wholeness always. -Lori

One

What is Magick?

*"You are the crowning glory.
Remember your splendor."*
– Laurence Galian

Magick is energy. The energy of all Life. It is Light, it is fluid. Magick moves, penetrates, encompasses all life forms.

Many people are conditioned to instantly associate Magick with parlor tricks, deceit, and a fun pass time that is commonly known as, magic.

When I was a little girl, it was easier to question/doubt less and accept all the real Magick in and around me.

In a sense everything we think and do is an act of Magick. For example. If we find ourselves thinking badly about ourselves often that is what Magick will manifest in and around us. If we think positive things about yourselves and others, you will manifest another kind of Magick.

Am I saying that magick is so simple that all we must do is to think of what we want, and we will get it? Yes and No.

There are two main types of magick. Light and Dark.

Dark magick corrupts, steals, uses, misleads/deceives, and will use the Magicker themselves, stripping them of Truth, Love, and Life. Leaving a void. Though dark magick is capable of manifesting desires, in the long run its main outcome is destruction.

Light Magick is drawn from the Source/Creator. Light magick heals and enlightens as users apply and explore it. It will lead those who are ready to new levels of enlightenment, and possibilities. It has no ego and is based in Love. The more we apply Light Magick to our walk the brighter colors become. Hopes, dreams, and possibilities come alive.

Is it easy? Yes and no. Light Magickers' are warriors. Just like becoming a Master of anything, exercise, becoming a great writer, parent, artist, etc., it takes time, effort, tears, laughter, and dedication. We make mistakes along the way. There will be times when your relationship with magick and the Divine will flow easily and harmoniously. Other times you may feel you have hit a wall or been hit by a wall. You may find yourself lost or distracted along the way.

Keep going. Magick itself will aid you. The Divine's ability to be ever present, loving, willing to help and heal is the most important reality I have found in this Life.

"Not by power not by might but by My Spirit says the Lord."

–Zechariah 4

What is a Spirit? Spirit is Magickal. Spirit is a living, conscious energy that connects body, heart, and mind. It also allows us to connect to the same energy that connects all life forms in this universe. Think of a tree root system. "All the trees here, and in every forest that is not too damaged, are connected to each other through underground fungal networks. Trees share water and nutrients through the networks and use them to communicate." – Richard Grant

There is no distance in the Spirit.

Life is Magick. It is the thoughts we think, and that act's we do. We are always choosing the light or dark path if we realize it or not. Acts of kindness are Light Magick and generate and build Lighter in our world and in the doer of the good act directly. The same happens as we use negative and selfish thoughts and acts. The more often dark Magick is used the more darkness grows within us and our world.

Magick is unavoidable.

Two

Connecting to the Divine

" You do not need to work to become spiritual.
You are spiritual; you need only to remember that fact.
Spirit is within you. God is within you."
— Julia Cameron

Realize the Divine is everywhere. Omnipotent and omnipresent.

The Divine isn't a place far away or hard to reach, and how to connect is through *acknowledgment*. God is always present. Only disbelief, deceit, fear, worry can take us away from the Divine Holy presence.

Close your eyes and take a few deep breaths and focus your intent/mind upon meeting or deepening your connection to the Divine. If possible, sit aligned with your back straight and feet on the ground (barefoot outside is best but not necessary for all spiritual work) and say, "I believe, I feel the Divine Spirit here with me now."

To fully connect to the Divine, you must *genuinely* want to. I suggest taking at least 5-10 minutes every morning to take the time to acknowledge and connect to the Divine. Making this a *priority* on a regular basis will indeed change your life in ways you may have never imagined. I've found when I take the time in the morning, throughout the day and before sleep to align with the Divine things flow quicker.

Remember the Divine is Holy and Pure. There is no bad intention within the Divine Source. It has unlimited layers of upliftment that never end. To be lifted higher and higher in Spirit means to be a better servant to humanity and ALL life forms.

Think of the Divine as your best friend and most trusted ally. Spend time talking and drawing closer to the Source as you would any family member or friend. Confide in and trust the Divine. The Divines guidance, gifts and intentions are pure and trustworthy. More importantly It is wiser and has unlimited knowledge and understanding – compared to any found from humanity alone.

A close relationship with the Divine creates Love. Do not be surprised if you find yourself realizing just how loved you are as you become closer to God.

You do not have to beg God. The Divine loves you unconditionally and truly desire the best for you.

When you seek Love, Wisdom, Truth, Goodness, Sanity, and Peace you are seeking the Divine.

Try getting an uplifting devotional to use often that resonates with you. Journaling your journey is always a good way to help spiritual growth and open your own gifts and consciousness.

Three

Your Divine Purpose

If you're on a journey to find your true purpose, and highest self, you are seeking the Divine and you are a being of Light and Love.

Invite the Holy Spirit to guide you. In other words, ask. Many people use the word, 'prayer' to define their communication with God.

Here is a simple prayer example, "Holy Divine please cleanse me of anything holding me back from my highest Divine purpose. Teach me to see and hear the Divines voice and guidance that is beyond myself and this world. Reveal my Divine Spiritual gifts to me. To know and understand the Holy Spirits presence within me and with me. Let the path open before me that leads me to my best self and purpose. I am grateful, thank You."

The important part is that what you ask for is genuine and from the heart. Trust that you are heard and growing even when you don't see or feel it happening.

Realize that there is a battle around us that is unseen for most but still very active. *"Our struggle is not against flesh and blood, but against the rulers, against the authorities, against the powers of this dark world and against the spiritual forces of evil in the heavenly realms."* – *Ephesians 6:12*

As you grow, you very well may face some obstacles, and adversity. Often adversity makes us question the Divine. It can also derail us and set us back years if we are not carefully guarded. You will also make countless choices without even realizing most of them as you traverse along your path.

Your relationship with the Divine and other Light workers will change your life forever.

Spiritual Gifts & Abilities

Wisdom
Knowledge
Faith
Healing
Working of Miracles
Prophecy
Discernment
Distinguishing spirits
Tongues, and Interpretation of Tongues

Psychic Abilities:

Astral projection or *mental projection* – The ability to voluntarily project an astral body or mental body, being associated with the out-of-body experience, in which one's consciousness is felt to temporarily separate from the physical body.

Autokinesis – The ability to control weather such as calling rainfall or storms.

Automatic writing – The ability to draw or write without conscious intent.

Bilocation – The ability to be present in two different places at the same time, usually attributed to a saint.

Cryokinesis – The ability to control ice or cold with one's mind.

Energy medicine – The ability to heal with one's own empathic, etheric, astral, mental or spiritual energy.

Ergokinesis – The ability to influence the movement of energy, such as electricity, without direct interaction.

Hydrokinesis – The ability to control water with one's mind.

Iddhi – Psychic abilities gained through Buddhist meditation.

<u>Inedia</u> – The ability to survive without eating or drinking, multiple cases have resulted in starvation or dehydration.

Invisibility – The ability to turn oneself invisible.

Illusions – The ability to conjure up illusions from one's mind.

<u>Levitation</u> or *transvection* – The ability to float or fly by mystical means.

<u>Materialization</u> – The creation of <u>objects</u> and <u>material</u> or the appearance of <u>matter</u> from unknown sources.

<u>Mediumship</u> or *channeling* – The ability to communicate with spirits.

<u>Petrification</u> – The power to turn a living being to stone by looking them in the eye.

Phytokinesis – The ability to control plants with one's mind.

<u>Prophecy</u> – (also *prediction, premonition, or prognostication*) — the ability to foretell events, without using induction or deduction from known facts.

Psychic surgery - The ability to remove disease or disorder within or over the body tissue via an "energetic" incision that heals immediately afterwards.

Pyrokinesis - The ability to control flames, fire, or heat using one's mind.

Psychic Hold - The ability to throw an electric current as if it is a rope.

Shapeshifting or *transformation* - The ability to physically transform the user's body into anything.

Telekinesis or *Psychokinesis* - The ability to influence a physical system without physical interaction, typically manifesting as being able to exert force, control objects and move matter with one's mind.

Teleportation - The ability is the hypothetical transfer of matter or energy from one point to another without

traversing the physical space between
them.

Thoughtography – The ability to impress
an image by 'burning' it on a surface
using one's own mind only.

Time Travel – The ability to escape the
flow of time by jumping to either the past
or the future.

Witnessing – The gift of being visited by
high profile spiritual beings such
as Mary, Jesus.

Xenoglossy – The ability of a person to
suddenly learn to write and speak a
foreign language without any natural
means such as studying or research, but
that is often rather bestowed by divine
agents.

Extrasensory perception, or *sixth sense* –
is an ability in itself as well as comprising
a set of abilities.

Clairvoyance – The ability to see things
and events that are happening far away,

and locate objects, places, people, using a <u>sixth sense</u>.

<u>Dowsing</u> - The ability to locate water, sometimes using a tool called a *dowsing rod*.

<u>Dermo-optical perception</u> - The ability to perceive unusual sensory stimuli through one's own skin.

<u>Dream telepathy</u> - The ability to telepathically communicate with another person through dreams.

<u>Precognition</u> (including psychic <u>premonitions</u>) - The ability to perceive or gain knowledge about future events, without using induction or deduction from known facts.

<u>Psychometry</u> or *psychoscopy* - The ability to obtain information about a person or an object by touch.

<u>Remote viewing</u> - *telesthesia* or *remote sensing* – The ability to see a distant or unseen target using extrasensory perception.

Retrocognition or *postcognition* – The ability to supernaturally perceive past events.

Telepathy – The ability to transmit or receive thoughts supernaturally.

Four

Becoming a Master

In the hidden realms where spirit and matter dance, the path to mastery unfolds. Like a muscle growing stronger through dedicated training, the soul expands its power through consistent spiritual practice.

Envision your consciousness as a vessel, small and delicate at first. Each meditation, each compassionate act, each moment of awareness enlarges this vessel. You begin by holding a mere drop of divine essence, but as you persist, your capacity grows. Soon you contain a stream, then a river, and ultimately an ocean of cosmic energy.

Ancient wisdom speaks of chi, prana, life force – energy flowing through all things. As you attune to it, you become a conduit. A martial artist, after years of practice, can break bricks with a touch. Similarly, you can learn to channel universal power.

Buddhist teachings describe the gradual illumination of mind. Imagine a dark room where each mindful act lights a candle. At first, you barely see, but as you continue, more candles ignite. Eventually, the room blazes with light, revealing reality's true nature.

Christ taught of the kingdom within. This inner realm is reached through patient cultivation. It's like tending a garden - daily removing weeds of negativity, planting seeds of love, watering with devotion. In time, your inner landscape blossoms with enlightenment.

Alchemists sought to turn lead into gold - a powerful metaphor for spiritual transformation. Your base consciousness, through the fire of practice and catalyst of grace, slowly becomes the gold of awakened awareness.

The journey of a thousand miles starts with one step. Each moment of practice builds on the last. Like a painter creating a masterpiece stroke by stroke, you craft your enlightened self with each mindful breath, loving thought, and selfless action.

As you progress, you'll discover the power you seek wells up from within. It's your true nature, your Buddha nature, your Christ consciousness, awakening to itself.

Mastering yourself, you master the universe, for they are one and the same.

Five

Meditation

The art of meditation is the key that unlocks the door to your inner sanctuary. Like a skilled diver plunging into the depths of the ocean, each time you meditate, you dive deeper into the vast expanse of your consciousness. At first, the waters may seem murky, filled with the flotsam of daily thoughts and worries. But with consistent practice, the waters clear, revealing the luminous pearl of your true nature.

Meditation is akin to tuning a fine instrument. Initially, your mind may be discordant, filled with chaotic thoughts. But as you sit in stillness, day after day, you begin to tune the strings of your awareness. Gradually, the cacophony fades, replaced by a harmonious symphony of inner peace.

Consider the lotus flower, a symbol of enlightenment in many Eastern traditions. It grows from the mud, yet emerges pristine and beautiful. Similarly, through meditation, you rise above the muck of mundane concerns, blossoming into your highest self.

As you cultivate your practice, you become like a mountain – solid, unshakeable, serene. The winds of circumstance may howl around you, but your inner core remains tranquil and unmoved. This steadiness becomes a refuge not only for yourself but for all who encounter you.

Here's a simple meditation to begin your journey:

Sit comfortably, spine straight but relaxed. Close your eyes and bring your attention to your breath. Feel the air entering and leaving your nostrils. As thoughts arise, acknowledge them without judgment, then gently return your focus to the breath. Start with just five minutes, gradually increasing the duration as you become more comfortable.

In the words of Thich Nhat Hanh from "Living Buddha, Living Christ," we can use simple phrases to anchor our mindfulness:

"Breathing in, I calm my body.

Breathing out, I smile.

Dwelling in the present moment,

I know this is a wonderful moment."

Remember, each breath is an opportunity to cultivate peace, each moment a chance to awaken. Through patient, persistent practice, you open the flower of your consciousness, revealing the Buddha, the Christ, the divine spark that has always dwelled within you.

Meditation:

1. Sit comfortably in a quiet place
2. Focus on your breath
3. When thoughts arise, gently return focus to breathing
4. Start with 5-10 minutes daily, gradually increase

Raising energy:

1. Visualize bright light entering your body
2. Practice deep, rhythmic breathing
3. Try gentle movements like swaying or arm raises
4. Feel the energy building from your core outward

Chanting examples:

1. "Om" - basic Sanskrit syllable, believed to be the sound of the universe
2. "Om Mani Padme Hum" - Tibetan Buddhist mantra for compassion
3. "Hare Krishna" - Hindu mantra for devotion

4. "Nam-myoho-renge-kyo" –
   Nichiren Buddhist chant for
   enlightenment

To practice:

1. Choose a chant that resonates with you
2. Repeat it slowly and clearly
3. Focus on the sound and vibration
4. Start with 5-10 minutes, gradually increase

Combining these practices can help calm the mind, increase focus, and cultivate a sense of inner peace and energy.

 Six

Aura/Life Field

"The energetic charge that is strongest in your electromagnetic field, also known as your aura or light body, is constantly attracting more of itself."
— *Amy Leigh Mercree*

The Aura along with Chakra's are an *energy field* that surrounds your entire body. Have you ever been around someone and just got a 'vibe'? You are most likely sensing someone's Aura.

Science refers to the Aura as the L-Field or Life Field.

1st Layer: Etheric
- Closest to the physical body
- Represents the physical body

- Connected to the root chakra
    - A bluish grey color
- Easiest to see with the naked eye
- Pulsates at 20 cycles per minute
- Stronger in those who are highly active
- Weaker in those who lead a sedentary lifestyle

2nd Layer: Emotional
- Second from the physical body
- Represents emotions and feelings
- Connected to the sacral chakra
- Can be all the colors of the rainbow
- Can be muddy colored during times of emotional stress
- State of the chakras can be easily determined from this layer

3rd Layer: Mental
- Third from the physical body

- Represents thoughts, cognitive processes, and state of mind

- Bright yellow in color
- Connected to the Solar plexus Chakra
- Radiates the strongest around the head, neck, and shoulders
- Stronger in those who engage in mental tasks, or deep thinkers
- When engaging in a creativity, energy sparks flow from this layer

4th Layer: Astral
- Fourth from the physical body
- Represents where we form our astral cords and connections with others
- Pink or rosy in color
- Connected to the heart chakra
- Stronger through loving, intimate relationships
- Weaker during hurtful breakups or conflicts with loved ones
- State of the chakras are easily visible from this layer

5th Layer: Etheric Template
- Fifth from the physical body
- Represents the entire blueprint of the body that exists on this physical plane
- Includes everything you create on this physical level, your identity, personality, and energy
- Connected to the throat chakra
- Varies in color
- Healed and made stronger by truth, knowing who you truly are and expressing it in healthy ways

6th Layer: Celestial
- Sixth from the physical body
- Connected to the third eye chakra
- Carries a strong and powerful vibration
- Represents the connection to the Divine and all beings
- Where unconditional love and unity flow
- Pearly white in color

- Assists in the ability to communicate with the spirit world and receive angelic messages
- Healed with unconditional love

7th Layer: Ketheric Template
- Furthest away from the physical body (est. around 2-3 ft.)
- Being one with the Universe
- Remembers all the information about your soul and previous lifetimes
- Vibrates at the highest frequency
- Connected to the crown chakra
- Gold in color
- Rapidly pulsates
- Assists with the ability to surrender to the path of the Divine, increases psychic abilities

Seeing your own Aura

1. Put your hand up in front of your face, spread your fingers wide and unfocus your eyes. Stare at your hand for several minutes.

2. Rub your index fingers together and look for color between them. Press and rub your index fingers together. After about 10 seconds, move your fingers apart, leaving about a 1/2 inch of space between them—the energy will "hang" between your fingers and you may be able to make out a colored mist.

- If you are having trouble concentrating, try sitting in a dimly lit room and meditating before you try this exercise.
- With continued practice, you will be able to see your and other peoples aura more clearly.

<u>Seven</u>

<u>Chakra's & the Full Armor of God</u>

"Put on the full armor of God, so that when the day of evil comes, you may be able to stand your ground, and after you have done everything, to stand. Stand firm then, with the belt of truth buckled around your waist, with the breastplate of righteousness in place, and with your feet fitted with the readiness that comes from the gospel of peace. In addition to all this, take up the shield of faith, with which you can extinguish all the flaming arrows of the evil one. Take the helmet of salvation and the sword of the Spirit, which is the word of God." Ep 6:8-10

Chakras, meaning "wheel" or "disk" in Sanskrit, are portals through which the main energetic channels of the body flow. There are seven chakras.

<u>Muladhara Chakra – Root Chakra</u> - The Root Chakra symbol consists of a 4-petalled lotus flower, a square, and a downward-facing triangle. Each element is said to represent the 4 aspects of the human mind, uniting to form the birth of the human consciousness.

Color: Red

Element: Earth

Location: The Root Chakra, also known as the Muladhara Chakra is located at the base of the spine, between the anus and the genitals. It is characterized by the emotions of survival, stability, ambition, and self-sufficiency.

Symptoms of a blocked Root Chakra: When this chakra is out of balance, a person starts feeling unstable, ungrounded, lack of ambition, lack of purpose, fearful, insecure, and frustrated.

Signs of a balanced/imbalanced Root Chakra: However, when the Root Chakra is balanced, these are replaced by more positive emotions, and you feel stable, confident, balanced, energetic, independent, and strong.

Mantra: The seed mantra (beej mantra) of Muladhara Chakra is 'Lam'.

2. Svadhishthana Chakra – Sacral Chakra

- The symbol for the Svadhishthana Chakra or Sacral Chakra is made up of multiple circles, a crescent moon, and six lotus flower petals. The circles and crescent moon represent the cyclical nature of life, death, and rebirth, while the 6 petals portray the 6 negative aspects of our nature that we need to overcome to open this chakra.

Color: Orange

Element: Water

Location: The Svadhishthana Chakra, more commonly known as the Sacral Chakra, is in the lower abdomen, about four fingers below the navel. Its attributes include the basic need for sexuality, as well as creativity and self-worth.

Symptoms of a blocked/imbalanced Sacral Chakra: When the Sacral Chakra is imbalanced, a person may feel emotionally explosive and irritable, sense a lack of energy and creativity, feel manipulative, or obsessed with sexual thoughts.

Signs of a balanced Sacral Chakra: When balanced, it makes one feel more vibrant, happy, positive, satisfied, compassionate, and intuitive.

Mantra: The seed mantra (beej mantra) of Svadhishthana Chakra is 'Vam'.

3. Manipura Chakra – Solar Plexus Chakra - The Solar Plexus Chakra symbol consists of a downward-pointing triangle within a ten-petalled lotus flower. The ten petals symbolize ten negative character traits that we must conquer, while the triangle is the Agni tattva or fire of

kundalini energy which signifies our inner strength.

Color: Yellow

Element: Fire

Location: The Manipura Chakra is located at the solar plexus, between the navel and the bottom of the rib cage. Characterized by emotions like ego, anger, and aggression.

Symptoms of a blocked/imbalanced Solar Plexus Chakra: An imbalance of the Solar Plexus Chakra can manifest physically as digestive problems, liver problems, or diabetes. On an emotional level, one might struggle with depression, lack of self-esteem, anger, and perfectionism.

Signs of a balanced Solar Plexus Chakra: By balancing this chakra, we feel more energetic, confident, productive, and focused.

Mantra: The seed mantra (beej mantra) of Manipura Chakra is 'Ram.'

4. Anahata Chakra – Heart Chakra - In the Heart Chakra symbol, two triangles intersect to form a yantra which represents the balance of yin and yang, or upward and downward forces. Outside, there is a lotus flower with 12 petals symbolizing the twelve divine qualities associated with the heart.

Color: Green

Element: Air

Location: As the name implies, the Anahata Chakra is in the heart region. This chakra is the seat of balance, and is characterized by emotions of love, attachment, compassion, trust, and passion.

Symptoms of a blocked/imbalanced Heart Chakra: When the heart chakra is imbalanced, a person may deal with emotional issues like anger, lack of trust, anxiety, jealousy, fear, and moodiness.

Signs of a balanced Heart Chakra: By harmonizing this energy center, a person begins to feel more compassionate, caring, optimistic, friendly, and motivated.

Mantra: The seed mantra (beej mantra) of Anahata Chakra is 'Yam'.

5. Vishuddha Chakra – Throat Chakra –

The symbol of the Throat Chakra consists of a 16-petalled lotus flower surrounding an inverted triangle which holds a circle within. This represents spiritual growth and the purification of the body, mind, and spirit.

Color: Blue

Element: Space

Location: The Visuddha Chakra is located at the base of the throat, coinciding with the thyroid gland. It is associated with inspiration, healthy expression, faith, and the ability to communicate well.

Symptoms of a blocked/imbalanced Throat Chakra: A blockage in the throat chakra may be experienced as timidity, quietness, a feeling of weakness, or the inability to express our thoughts.

Signs of a balanced Throat Chakra: When this chakra is balanced, it enables creativity, positive self-expression, constructive communication, and a sense of satisfaction.

Mantra: The seed mantra (beej mantra) of Vishuddha Chakra is 'Ham'.

<u>6. Ajna Chakra – Third Eye Chakra</u> - The Third Eye Chakra symbol consists of an inverted triangle resting in a circle between two lotus petals. The two petals and downward-facing pyramid both

signify wisdom, emphasizing the Third Eye Chakra's role in our journey to spiritual awareness.

Color: Indigo

Element: None

Location: The Ajna Chakra (pronounced as 'Agya Chakra') is located between the eyebrows. Also known as the Third Eye Chakra, it is often used as a focal point during asana practice to develop more concentration and awareness. It is said that meditating upon this chakra destroys the karma of past lives and brings liberation and intuitive knowledge. Its attributes are intelligence, intuition, insight, and self-knowledge.

Symptoms of a blocked/imbalanced Third Eye Chakra: When imbalanced, it may make you feel non-assertive and afraid of success, or on the contrary, it can make you more egotistical. An imbalance can manifest as physical problems like headaches, blurry vision, and eye strain. **Signs of a balanced Third Eye Chakra:** When this chakra is active and balanced, a person feels more vibrant and confident, both spiritually and emotionally. In the absence of the fear of death, one becomes his own master and remains free of all attachment to material things. **Mantra:** The seed mantra (beej mantra) of Ajna Chakra is 'Om'.

7. Sahastrara Chakra – Crown Chakra -

The Crown Chakra symbol is depicted as a ring of a thousand lotus petals surrounding an inverted triangle. This symbolizes the rising of divine energy into the Crown Chakra, bringing spiritual liberation and enlightenment.

Color: Violet White

Element: None

Location: The Sahastrara or Crown Chakra is located at the crown of the head. The seventh chakra is the center of spirituality, enlightenment, and dynamic thought and energy. It allows for the inward flow of wisdom and brings the gift of cosmic consciousness.

Symptoms of a blocked/imbalanced Crown

Chakra: When it gets imbalanced, one might suffer from a constant sense of frustration, melancholy, and destructive feelings.

Signs of a balanced Crown Chakra: A balanced Crown Chakra promotes spiritual understanding, inner peace and a clear perspective on the world.

Mantra: The seed mantra (beej mantra) of Sahastrara Chakra is 'Aum'.

The Full Armor of God

1. **Shoes with the preparation of the gospel of peace** - Root "I Am."

2. **The Belt of Truth** - Sacral (Svadhishthana) Chakra "I Feel."

3. **The Shield of Faith** - Plexus (Manipura) Chakra "I Will—I Can—I Do."

4. **Breastplate of Righteousness** - the Heart (Anahata) Chakra "I Love."

5. **The Sword of the Spirit** - the Word of God, is my source of Truth,

corresponding to the Throat
(Vishuddha) Chakra "I Speak."

6. **<u>The Helmet of Salvation</u>** - restores
me to wholeness, corresponding to
the Third (Ajna) Eye—Spiritual Eye
Chakra "I See."

7. **<u>The Helmet of Salvation</u>** - restores
me to wholeness, also
corresponding to the Crown
(Sahasrara) Chakra. "I Know—I
Understand."

8.

Armor of God + Chakra Meditation
by HEATHER WIEST [1]

"Place hands on the feet. Take a few, deep breaths.

Oh Lord, I put on The Shoes of Peace, corresponding to the Root (Muladara) Chakra "I Am."
Color—Red
Element—Earth

I am a child of God, Your beloved. My foundation is in Jesus Christ, my Lord and Savior. I let go of any fear or doubt and walk in bold faith and trust. I am grounded, safe, and secure. I seek peace wherever I go. You direct my steps. I am willing to move forward through divine healing and guidance.

Place hands on the belly. Take a few, deep belly breaths.

The Belt of Truth wraps around me, corresponding to the Sacral (Svadhishthana) Chakra "I Feel."
Color—Orange
Element—Water

Oh God, Your Truth has brought freedom into my life. I feel my spiritual core stability. I radiate joy, creativity, and balance. As I am intimate with You, I am able to be intimate with others in healthy ways. I trust the divine flow of life. I let Your Spirit move me.

Place arms crossed over the chest. Take a few, deep breaths.

The Shield of Faith protects me, corresponding to the Solar Plexus (Manipura) Chakra "I Will—I Can—I Do." Color—Yellow
Element—Fire

I can do all things through Christ who gives me strength! When I let the Spirit work in and through me, I have stamina, self-discipline, and confidence. My body is full of energy, health, and vitality. Thank you, Lord, for this weapon which enables me to thwart fiery darts in the spiritual realm. I am able to encourage and hold space for others as we link our Shields of Faith.

Place hands on the heart space. Take a few, deep breaths.

Jesus (Yeshua Ben Josef), You are my divine center, the Breastplate of Righteousness, corresponding to the Heart (Anahata) Chakra "I Love."

I love because You first loved me. I forgive because I have been forgiven. I am compassionate, joyful, and connected to others. I can trust and be trustworthy. I am capable of establishing, growing, and maintaining healthy relationships.

Place hands lightly on the throat area. Take a few, deep breaths.

The Sword of the Spirit, the Word of God, is my source of Truth, corresponding to the Throat (Vishuddha) Chakra "I Speak."

Out of the heart I speak. Thank you, God, for the beautiful visual of the top of the breastbone looking like a sword handle pulling truth out of the heart, moving up to the mouth, and into the world as expression. This is the only offensive weapon in the Armor of God! I ask that you fill me with Your Truth and help me to discern and deny any lies in myself, others, and the world. May my words speak truth and life. Please help me to be an attentive, receptive listener. May my communications be clear, effective, and impactful.

Place Anjali mudra (prayer) hands at the brow center. Take a few deep breaths.

The Helmet of Salvation restores me to wholeness, corresponding to the Third (Ajna) Eye—Spiritual Eye Chakra "I See."

Oh Lord, thank you for enlightening my spiritual eyes to receive divine knowledge and wisdom. Jesus, You save, heal, and restore me! My wholeness is secure in You. I quiet my busy mind by closing my physical eyes, and tuning into Your Presence, Love and Light. I see the interconnectedness of life and am filled with vibrant clarity and focus. Your visions inspire me to make a difference and encourage others.

Place hands on the top of the head. Take a few deep breaths.

The Helmet of Salvation restores me to wholeness, also corresponding to the Crown (Sahasrara) Chakra.

"I Know—I Understand."

Color—Violet

Element—Thought

I am fully connected spiritually and have access to divine wisdom and understanding. God, I can call on You at any time—and You hear my thoughts and petitions. Through prayer and meditation, You show me Your higher purposes, and I notice Your Divine work in everything. I desire to know You more! I am calm, centered, and complete in You, Oh Lord."

"Just like the Crown Chakra represents our connection to God, I believe Jesus is our connection to God. He is the bridge between God and man. I can know and understand His Presence personally and intimately. This is the source of my higher purpose. When I mentally and spiritually dress myself in the full Armor of God, and cleanse and clear the Chakra energy centers of my body, I feel fully connected and empowered to LOVE, SERVE, and INSPIRE! "– <u>HEATHER WIEST</u> [1]

---

[1] 1. Heather Weist - https://loveserveinspire.com/2018/11/09/armor-of-god-chakra-meditation/

Eight

Cleansing & Charging

"A person might be an expert in any field of knowledge or a master of many material skills and accomplishments. But without inner cleanliness his brain is a desert waste."

–Sri Sathya Sai Baba

Cleansing

Energy is known to build and needs to be cleansed just like any object, room or being. Spiritual energy is always there but rarely seen.

It's easy to see the cobwebs and dust building in the house or our skin getting sweaty after a long day. Spiritual energy isn't so easy to identify or notice but its equally important to keep the spiritual energy within and around us clean too.

Cleansing means getting rid of all energy good and bad.

Items, such as crystals, or any tools used, will also gather energy, and need to be cleansed. Remember, cleansing will not hold good energy forever. If you want to add good energy, you need to charge.

Cleansing can be done using the Divine Spirit, plants, smoke, the elements, and intention/visualization. Intention is the most important part of any spiritual practice.

Focus on what you are cleansing, and with a sense of respect, focus on what you want the cleansing to do. As you are thinking about that, light some incense, or sage and wave it around what you wish to clear off energy or use whatever tools you desire.

There are many ways to cleanse, find what works well for you.

<u>Charging</u>

After we have cleansed ourselves, our stones/gems, our tools, our space we often do not think of refilling it with energy. Purposeful energy.

Charging is exactly that. Energy drawn for a purpose.

A charge can be made to increase spiritual connections or simply to raise the power of an object for our own use.

We all have an inner self that needs charging. Charging can increase our own focus on life.

There are several ways to charge including, channeling the Holy Spirit/Divine (visualize pure Light filling yourself/the object or space), using the Sun or Moon, using any element, and self-will/intent.

My favorite ways are immersing myself in a quiet place with the Divine Spirit. Channeling and visualizing the Divine energy flowing through myself and anything I am working with. I love to incorporate the Cardinal Points/Elements in all my work.

Practice until you find what is best for you.

Nine

Protection

Have you ever been near someone who drains you? Walked into a room and felt a change in atmosphere? Or turned your head to see someone staring at you? If you have answered yes to one or all of these, then you have experienced your body's spiritual energy system at work.

Through your body's spiritual energy system, you can sense, feel, and intuit everything and everyone you encounter.

Flowing within and around your physical body is a subtle energy field known as the aura or scientifically, the Life Field or L-Field.

Your aura is a kaleidoscope of electromagnetic energy. Your aura is not just colored energy it is a complex and remarkable structure constantly sending, receiving, and absorbing energy exchanges with everyone and everything you encounter. It is because of this invisible and silent energetic interplay that you can sense, tune, and feel the world around you.

Here are tools and techniques that will help you to protect your spiritual energy as well as cleanse and re-energize it.

1. Power words

Power words are incredibly easy and effective tools to use in a situation where you would like to protect yourself energetically, emotionally, and mentally. All these aspects of being are closely interwoven. As the name suggests, a power word is a word that has a vast amount of meaning and symbolism. It has a very specific energy attached to it.

Words like love, om or peace are all great power words but there are many more. Often your power word is the opposite to what is happening. If someone is irritating you, your power word could be calm. If you are being drained, focus on the word invincible, whereas if feeling dark, concentrate on the word light.

Whatever power word feels right for that given moment just hold it in the forefront of your awareness. Connect with the energy of the word as fully as you can allowing its vibrational frequency to ripple out through every cell and fiber of your being and out into your aura. Feel or imagine the effect of the word on your mind, body, heart, soul, and spiritual energy systems. You can repeat the word silently over and over if this helps you to focus. It is unbelievably quick and can restore and recenter your spiritual energy, mindset, and emotions in a few moments.

2. Breathe in your power

Life is full of moments that can cause us to feel overwhelmed, stressed, and reactive. These triggers can throw your energy and disturb your peace and every emotion. Every state we feel is mirrored within our aura. Love and happiness strengthens our aura whereas anger depletes and weakens it. This simple breath technique is useful to know as it can instantly rebalance mind, body, spirit, and spiritual energy.

Simply close your mouth and breathe gently through your nose. Allow your attention to flow with your breath in and out of the body. Notice the rise and fall of your chest. Let your shoulders drop, relax your jaw all the while focusing on your breathing. Even just five slow, mindful breathes in and out work!

Research has proven that breath work alone has an instant and powerful effect on every part of your body and mind as well as your soul and energy systems. However, you can make it even more powerful by adding a creative visualization to it. Picture a beam of light shining down from the cosmos onto your head (or whatever higher power you believe in). Imagine that as you inhale you draw in this cosmic light to cleanse and energize you and on every exhalation, you breathe out and release any unwanted energy, stress, or negativity you are holding. Even just a few moments of breath work are transformational. Remember the more you practice these the easier and more

intuitive exercises like this become.
Becoming a Master.

3. Seal off your spiritual energy field

This exercise enable you to seal off your aura and protect yourself from any person, situation, or environment. All you need to do is imagine yourself standing inside a gigantic bubble which is clear, flexible, and impenetrable. The bubble encompasses you creating a powerful shield that moves with you.

You can play with this visualization and power it up by imaging that the top of the bubble is connected to the universe so that there is a flow of beautiful, cosmic energy entering your sacred space. You can change the color of your bubble using gold for a cosmic link, pink for love, blue for healing, or red for energy. In fact, you can add whatever elements that inspire you. There is a relative alive or in the spirit world you would like to imagine standing with you in your bubble whose presence empowers and strengthens you. You can even bring in your four-legged friends!

Another great visualization commonly used is a mirror. If you ever want to block the other persons energy touching your spiritual being, then imagine an enormous mirror popping up in front of you. All the energy being thrown towards you is deflected off from the mirror and back towards the source. Do not underestimate the power of creative visualizations. Research has shown that the act of imagining something in your mind's eye is equally powerful to physically doing it!

4. A cloak of protection

There are many times when it is useful to be able to protect your aura, such as when using public transport, attending busy offices or when around vexatious people. Simply visualize yourself in a full-length sweeping cloak that has been made from the darkest shade of blue – like the midnight blue of the night sky. This cloak has a hood, that you can imagine pulling up so that your head (crown chakra) is also protected. The lining of the cloak could be magical – pink, silver, golden or multicolored. It can be decorated on the inside and out with magical symbols. Whenever you feel the need to protect yourself and your energy from external influences pull on your cloak – this powerful visualization harnesses your creative forces and sets a clear energetic intention.

5. Nature's cure

The benefits of spending time in nature is immeasurable. Being in nature and grounding with her energy counters the effects of ageing and inflammation as well as cleansing and energizing the mind, body, and spirit. You will feel stronger and more anchored and in turn will power up your auric shield. If you can, try to make the time to walk by the sea, stroll in a park or stomp in a forest – and when you are there spare a conscious thought for the restorative energy exchanges taking place and the gift of nature's magick.

Another way you can refresh your aura is to ground yourself. This is a particularly great exercise if you spend a lot of time working, thinking and being in your head! Ideally done outdoors, take off your shoes place your feet flat on the ground (if you cannot get outside close your eyes and imagine that is where you are) Feel the connection of your feet to the ground and allow the energy of the earth to connect with your bodies energy system. If you want to add another powerful dimension to this grounding exercise imagine that the soles of your feet grow roots that burrow down deep into the earth. Through these roots you anchor down and quite literally ground yourself. Visualize an energy exchange taking place where your energy (both good and negative) flows out of you into the earth and in return Mother Earth's energy flows up through your roots and feet into your body circulating round your entire energy systems – cleansing, energizing, and restoring you. You might like to say a prayer of thanks to Mother Earth for her healing.

6. Cleansing

Your aura is constantly interacting with the world around you and in doing so energy exchanges are constantly occurring, not all of which are uplifting and positive. Knowing how to cleanse your aura means that it remains vibrant and energetically strong to protect you. Salt baths are an ideal way to do this and offer you the opportunity to set aside thirty/forty minutes for some spiritual self-care. This kind of bath will not need the usual products, just Epsom Salt.

- Put Epsom salt (2-3 good handfuls) into a regular bath. You can add essential oils like lavender if you know this works for you.
- As you do this set the intention that whilst bathing you will let go of all negativity that you are holding and carrying
- Ask the universe and or your spirit guides to guide you in cleansing and to help you realize your spiritual vibration.
- You can set the mood with incense, candles, crystals, and music.
- Use your breath to be still and center.
- Be mindful – notice what thoughts and feeling arise.

This bathing routine (once a month is about right) is a lovely way to look after your aura but to enjoy some quiet reflection. These moments are often the times when realizations and insights have the time to arise and be noticed.

7. Heavenly Protection

Many of us believe in angels and this exercise is a beautiful way to connect with this heavenly realm for yourself! Archangel Michael is one of the seven Archangels. Known to be a fierce, powerful warrior, he is regarded as the Prince of the Archangels. He brings forth the qualities of strength, courage, and protection. Simply by saying the words "Archangel Michael protect me now" you invoke or call on him.

You can just ask for his help or you can imagine that he comes and stands to the right-hand side of you with his sword and shield ever ready to guard and protect you. You can visualize him pulling his deep blue cloak around you, or you would like to imagine his wings wrapping around you to protect and shield you. This is especially lovely to do if you are sad or feeling emotionally fragile. How beautiful to imagine being scooped up and held in the protection and unconditional love of heaven's most powerful Archangel.

8. Love

Research in quantum physics, neuroscience, biophysics, and epigenetics are all revealing new and wondrous possibilities around science, spirituality, and man. What is emerging is that we have the power to create and sculpt our reality. You can begin to access this power for yourself through practices like meditation and mindfulness. These and other such spiritual pathways (practicing gratitude) can transform your life even down to your hard wiring and genetic makeup.

All the ancient spiritual practices of the world call us to love. Love is the most powerful energy that exists.

When we express our love even through kindness and compassion it radiates out from us not only into the people and world around us but far out into the universe. When you feel positive and loving your aura is vibrant and strong. Negativity is automatically deflected.

Your heart is your superpower when it comes to auric protection. It really is all about the love![2]

---

[2] https://earthmonk.guru/psychic-protection-for-empaths/

Ten

Element's & Elemental's

"Don't fear the light within.
May it ignite the Sacred Flame in your soul."

– Paulo Cohelo

The Five Elements

All Elements exist in, on, and above the Earth, which connects us to the Divine Source in a close bond.

Air — The East, sunrise/dawn, the **Spring Equinox**, Travel, Freedom, Knowledge, Communication, Mental Clarity, Intuition, Psychic Abilities, & Creativity, the early waxing Moon.

Like a breath of fresh Air brining's knowledge, wisdom and insight as this element moves through our lives. Air brings with it an opening of mind and sight as well as the new light of dawn and as such is the element to work with when you need to attain these things. This is the element of the scholar, but also of joy as it brings the rebirth of spring.

Direction – East
Time – Dawn
Season – Spring
Colors – Yellow, White, Pink
Magick – Knowledge, Wisdom
Tool – Censure/Incense or Wand (interchangeable with Sword)

Elemental – Sylphs are Air Elementals that grace the highest of realms, such as mountain tops. They ride the air currents viewing humanity from afar. They are whimsical but tend the forests and forests with great care.

Ruling Planets - Mercury, Jupiter, Uranus
Gemstones - Topaz, Pumice, Smokey Quartz, Sapphire, Lapis Lazuli, Labradorite, Kyanite

Fire — The **South**, noon,
the **Summer Solstice**, Protection,
Courage, Strength, Inspiration,
Purification, Confidence, Vitality,
Creativity, Passion, Change, the full
Moon, the Sun at its zenith.

Fire can be harmful and destructive as well as regenerative. Fire is also comforting and protecting, it drives away the darkness and gives us courage to face the darkest nights.

Direction – South
Time – Midday
Season – Summer
Colors – Red, Orange, Gold
Magick – Strength, Passion/Love, Anger, Regeneration, Protection
Tool – Sword or Wand

Elemental – Dragons and Djinn are spirits of Fire but the main elemental associated with it is the Salamander. Sometimes an amphibian of fire, more often a lizard, these creatures are born of fire and are most comfortable living in arid deserts or volcanos and lava lakes.

Ruling Planets – Mars, the Sun
Gemstones - Clear Quartz, Jasper, Fire Agate, Citrine, Sunstone, Carnelian, Ruby, Garnet.

Water — The West, sunset, the **Autumn Equinox**, Happiness, Cleansing, Dreams, Harmony, Love, Healing, Health, Divination, the waning Moon.

Water is all about emotions and the emotional aspects of life and Magick. It is closely associated with the moon, dreams and psychic abilities and is often used as a tool of divination. Air is associated with academic knowledge Water is associated with occult wisdom.

Direction – West
Time – Sunset
Season – Autumn
Colors – Blue, Silver, Turquoise, Yellow, White
Magick – Wisdom, Dreams, Emotions, Relationships, Psychic Development
Tool – Chalice

Elemental – Mermaids, Naiads and Oceanid are all types of Undines, water elementals that grace the waterways and oceans with their presence. They protect the waters in which they reside

Ruling Planets – Moon, Neptune
Gemstones - Aquamarine, Opal, Moonstone, Pearl, Chrysoprase, Kunzite, Blue Tourmaline, Amethyst

Earth – The **North**, night/midnight, the **Winter Solstice**, Money, Prosperity, Abundance, Confidence, Career Success, Grounding, Stability, Fertility, the veiled dark Moon.

The most fixed and stable of the magickal Elements; Earth is the tangible ground beneath our feet, the plants and animals that fill the world around us. When we need to feel stable and safe it is this element that we turn to ground ourselves.

Direction – North
Time – Midnight
Season – Winter
Colors – Black, Brown, Green
Magick – Fertility, Protection, Health, Financial
Tool – Pentacle

Elemental – Gnome, Brownies and Bucca are all types of Earth elementals, these magickal creatures are closely allied with the substance of the Earth or the natural world and in's inhabitants.

Ruling Planets – Saturn, Venus
Gemstones - Peridot, Emerald, Jade, Hematite, Malachite, Jet, Tourmaline, Granite, Onyx, Quartz, Amethyst

Spirit – All directions, all time, all seasons. Divine, infinity, purity, space, consciousness, perfection, holy, immaterial, aether/ether, Life Force, pure energy, unlimited potential.

The fifth element. It resides in all of it, central to our being and the spark from which we take life but it is also the spark of the Divine which we carry within ourselves.

Direction – No Direction – placed at the Centre or the point
Time – All Time and No Time
Colors – Purple, White
Magick – Psychic Development, Protection, Divinity, Higher Self
Tool – The Heart and Will, sometimes depicted as a spiral or an oval

Elemental – Spirit
Ruling Planet - Rules all Planets
Gemstones - All

Aether is a divine and indestructible substance. Its natural habitat is the Universe, where stars and other celestial bodies are created. Aether is understood as the soul of our reality and all life emanates from it.

Sylphs

Sylphs are an Air Elemental and often identified as faeries or even angels. The male version of a Sylph is a Zephyr.

They are spiritual creatures associated with the element of air and some believe, wood. They are particularly attuned to the wind, trees, and other forms of nature. Sylphs are known to appear as tiny sparks of light or transparent wispy beings moving rapidly from place to place.

You may have felt the Air spirits when you are out in nature feeling their wind pass over you or hearing their playful nature move and rustle through the trees and landscapes. I have found Air to be quite warm (at heart), caring and thoughtful.

The Sylph is beautiful, lively, and beneficent to human beings. They are known to be mirthfully changeable, and eccentric.
Poets and have described them leaving beautiful green rings in meadows and fields from dancing round and round.

Air elementals make up the mental plane of the Earth and serve to balance and maintain our weather systems. Sylphs help to inspire our thinking, bring solutions to problems, and assist in relieving stress through stimulating positive thought and creative ideas.

Air beings also assist in aligning both hemispheres of our brain so we can be both intuitive and rational at the same time. This helps to bring in intelligence and knowledge of the higher realms of existence without the interference of ego.

Ritual

Find a place outside or inside where you are near an open window or door. Take the time to center and relax. You may decorate your altar or sacred space to draw and honor Sylphs with leaves, dandelions, burning incense or sage, petals, acorns, or feathers. It's said that they like bright colors like yellow and white.

Wind chimes are also a great tool to use while communing with the Sylphs.

Using your inner voice ask the Sylphs to show themselves to you. It helps to relax your eyes, half closing them as if you are about to fall into a cozy trance. Open your heart and mind as you gaze at the sky. You may start to see flickers of light or darting whites, grays, and blacks or other colors of energy.

To connect on a deeper level to the Air Elementals use breathing and mindfulness techniques daily or on a regular basis.

For example, take several moments to acknowledge Air at the start of your day. Take slow, deep breaths. Breathing in the intelligent, Light energy of Air. As you breathe in, allow your entire being to be filled with Air. Feel and visualize it expanding within and through you. Realize you are present in the current moment. Allow yourself to be okay and content. Each exhale leave the worries and stress behind.

Next, set your intention/hope for the day. "Today will be extra joyful and easy going." Or "I will be extra creative today." "I will affect others with my positivity." The possibilities in Magick are endless.

<u>18 Ways to connect to
Air Elementals</u>

- Feel the wind on your skin
- Cloud watching
- Fly a kite or put out pinwheels
- Practice divination
- Watch the sun rise
- Put out a bird feeder
- Burn incense or sage/bay leaves etc.
- Perform visualization meditations
- Put up wind chimes
- Enjoy the wind outside on an extra windy day
- Read something/fertilize your mind
- Go for a hot air ballon ride
- Hike up a mountain and appreciate the change in air up there
- Start your day with positive affirmations
- Inhale deeply, feeling the air fill your lungs and blood stream
- Reduce the ways you contribute to air pollution
- Grow/keep plants and or gardens
- Ask to Connect

Salamanders

Salamanders are associated with the Fire Element and like all Elemental Beings, are multidimensional. Salamanders live within every flame and are the personification of the Sun. They represent Divine Will and nurture the creative fire within.

The word Salamander means, from Old French salamandre, from Latin salamandra, from Greek σαλαμάνδρα, which is used for the fire salamander.

Salamanders work behind the scenes to keep our realm peaceful. An Elemental Salamanders appearance is similar to a normal the known salamander. A small lizard like a newt.

Every time you light a candle or build a fire you spark the presence of the Salamander who dwells within the Fires consciousness. Salamanders can help us to calm our inner storms.

Invoking Fire elementals can help us to burn away and purify all things that no longer (or never did) serve our highest purpose. Their main purpose as an Elemental is to promote self-healing and control of our own emotions.

Salamanders are wonderful at creating creative force to bring in the new. They help manifest enthusiasm, drive, will power, motivation, self-confidence, courage, creativity, unclouded vision, insight, and clairvoyance.

Physically they assist in balanced metabolism, core temperature, circulation, and increased energy.

Ways to honor the Salamander spirit and invite them into your magickal workings is through fire. A simple candle to a much larger scale fire (a campfire) will resonate with the Salamander. Decorating your alter or sacred space with colors such as yellow, orange, and red (or whatever colors that connect to Fire for you) to create a warm, inviting vibe.

Ritual

Find a comfortable, quiet place where you will not be disturbed. All you will need is a candle and a way to light your candle.

Sit comfortably facing the South and the candle. Take a moment to center, breathing in and out comfortably, slowly. Asking the Divine to guide all your workings.

When you are ready, light the candle asking the fire to bless your intentions and for healing.

Gaze deeply into the flame allowing yourself to connect to the Fire, becoming one.

Keep your gaze on the flame, think about anything you wish to release, clear, or heal from. Emotions, physical illness, unhealthy attachments, or anything you wish to be free of. As you think of these things, be willing to resolve anything that could be holding you back. Offer forgiveness, compassion, and love.

Breathe out all that you wish to let go of. Releasing it to the Divine and into the Fire for purification. Breathing out: letting go, breathing in you are filled with Love, Divine Fire, and strength.

When you are finished take the time to notice how you feel. Lighter, and more empowered? This is a great time to make notes in your journal also.

When you are reading as the Salamander Elemental to make itself known to you. Open your spirit and heart to sense their presence as they allow you to glimpse or behold them within the Flame.

It may take time or several tries before you experience knowing any elemental up close.

Get to know them, ask them questions, connect often, thank them for their gifts, energy, and guidance.

When you are ready you may blow out your candle or allow it to burn out itself. As you let it burn down or blow it out, visualize the work you just did manifesting with a sense of Love and gratitude.

18 Ways to Connect to Fire Elementals

- ➢ Soak in the Sunshine
- ➢ Light your fireplace or have a bonfire
- ➢ Create something new
- ➢ Face a fear
- ➢ Use candles for various rituals, meditations, and spells
- ➢ Start a passion project
- ➢ Open and really appreciate the beauty of Creation that surrounds you each day
- ➢ Honor the sun at noon on a bright, warm day
- ➢ Make a list of new goals
- ➢ Perform a cleansing ritual
- ➢ Watch a sunset or sunrise
- ➢ Think about your life; what energizes you and makes you feel passionate?
- ➢ Perform some glamour magick for a boost of confidence
- ➢ Say positive things to yourself on a daily basis
- ➢ Do something competitive or challenging
- ➢ Be bold and honest
- ➢ Make sun-water
- ➢ Ask to Connect

Undines

Undines are Elementals associated with Water. They are spiritual beings that share the physical plane. Undines are found in every drop of Water. Undines derive their name from the Latin word *unda*, meaning "wave." Their presence represents beauty and dreams.

They like to live in and protect the waterways and are relatively benign elementals, known to aid sailors in safe passage. They are the most linked to humans and their appearance can be that of beautiful angels and resemble human beings in appearance and size.

Undines have a special love for flowers and plants, which they serve almost as devotedly and intelligently as Gnomes. Undines work with the vital essence of plants and the liquids within the plants, animals, and human beings.

These watery creatures are almost exclusively female. Undines carry the traits of the Water Element including being emotional, intuitive, and often innocent.

Undines are intelligent, emotional, fond of serving mankind, friendly and helpful unless threatened.

Undines crave attention and are known to have amazing singing voices. They have been known to lure humans in while singing close to shores with they are ethereal song.

Undines have many forms and known by many names including, Ondine, Water Sprite, Naiad (who are said to live in fountains, streams, and wells), Nereids, Limoniades, Oreade, Nymph, Sea Maid, Mermaid, and Potamides.

Ritual

To invoke the elementals of Water in your practice, work with the cycles of the moon. Perform rituals on full and new moons. Of course, you can use this ritual any time or any day of the year.

This spell will assist you in connecting with an undine: a water elemental. Undines are able to provide emotional healing, the ability to delve deep into our subconscious, and a general feeling of emotional renewal. Invoke them when you feel depressed or lacking in passion.

The Water Elemental symbolizes cleaning and purification and is a fluid element in which, by immersion, metals are cleaned of all impurities.

Set up an altar with water at the center. Allow it to soak up the energy of the moon, creating Moon Water. After your Moon Water is ready, mindfully drink or bathe in the water the next day.

After you have drank or bathed in the Moon Water, (you can also alternatively save the Moon Water and drink it while you do this next spell ritual) set up your Alter and clear your Sacred Space. If possible, use a blue candle (white is a good medium if do not have blue), and set a bowl or glass of water in front of the candle on your altar.

Face the West, center and begin. Light your candle and begin to gaze through the Water so that you can see the candlelight through it until you feel yourself becoming one, fluid with the Water.

Greet the Undine/s within the Water. Thank them for their presence and all the good they have done for Earth and Humanity and for honoring the Divine.

Look into the Water with your inner sight. Allow the undines to reveal themselves to you. Once they have, you may commune with them as you wish.

<u>17 Ways to Connect to Water Elementals</u>

- ➢ Have a ritual bath or shower
- ➢ Collect seashells or snails
- ➢ Drink water often
- ➢ Moon bathe
- ➢ Make moon-water
- ➢ Watch, listen, or take a walk in the rain
- ➢ Visit a body of water/swim
- ➢ Collect rainwater
- ➢ Keep/grow water plants
- ➢ Do a cleansing of your space
- ➢ Start a dream journal
- ➢ Spend time outside at dusk
- ➢ Perform a moon meditation or ritual
- ➢ Don't hold back your feelings
- ➢ Practice water scrying
- ➢ Take a moonlit walk near water
- ➢ Ask to connect

Gnomes

Gnomes are protectors of the forest. Guardians of Earth energy. Messengers of Mother Nature. Both male and female Gnomes are powerful healers.

They are known to be about 1-2FT tall. Gnome children live at home with their parents until they are 100 years old when they're ready to take a mate and fend on their own. Gnome males often prefer female Gnome's on the chubbier side as partners. Gnome's live to be about 350-500 years.

Gnomes are found around dry leaves, tree bases, rock's, old logs, and mushrooms. Gnomes often live in woods, gardens, hills, and glens. Gnomes reside in the underbrush found in trees, roots, and soil. They can live in the mines of the earth or take care of the hidden treasures that lie there. Gnomes are the guardians of all treasures and precious metals hidden under mountains and deserts.

They enjoy staying hidden and observing. If one has ever been in your home, it may have appeared as a shadowy blur moving by. Gnomes are quick, smart, evasive, and curious.

Gnomes have Earth Magick secrets and wisdom to share with those who are ready. They connect easiest to people who love and protect nature, animals, and other healers.

Gnomes can help you with stability, grounding, or deep spiritual cleansing.

Ritual

So, are you ready to meet or connect to a Gnome?

If possible, find quiet place outdoors where you are able to feel safe and comfortable. Take a few moments to center, connect to the Earth, feel the air, the grass or dirt under you, listen to the sounds, and release all negative energy. Breathing in peaceful, clear energy.

Next, ask for the Gnome's trust. Make an offering (make sure you pack up all the items you plan to use before venturing out). Grab crystals, a new plant to care for, vegetables, blueberries, seeds, nuts, or other healing herbs.

Tell the Gnome's you are there in peace and would like to offer them this gift in return for their trust, friendship, wisdom, and protection. Ask how you could help to bring positive, free flowing energy through the Earth.

Take a moment, breathe, connect. Ask for healing guidance. Allow yourself to receive your message/'s intuitively. It is sure to be a blessing and benefit both yourself and the Earth.

Remember Gnomes are shy, playful, and love cold nature. Spending more quiet moments outside and repeatedly reaching out to the Gnomes in Spirit and continuing gift giving will increase your chance of a direct encounter.

Adding a Gnome statue to honor the Gnomes indicates to them that you also are a protector of the forest and all life there. You can also create an Earth alter in your home and/or in your yard somewhere.

Gnomes are Spiritual (metaphysical), physical, and dimensional beings.

Doing daily meditations/mantras/chants and practicing daily mindfulness will also increase your chances of direct contact with gnomes and most Magickal Beings that are Lightworkers.

14 Ways to Connect to Earth Elementals

- ➢ Start each day greeting Nature
- ➢ Be outside barefoot on the Earth
- ➢ Outdoor meditations or rituals
- ➢ Plant a garden
- ➢ Have plants inside your home
- ➢ Perform Kitchen Magick
- ➢ Visit the forest
- ➢ Appreciate the sights, sounds, and smells of nature
- ➢ Work on your root chakra
- ➢ Plant trees
- ➢ Collect stones, rocks, gems and use them in your practice
- ➢ Be aware and kind of animals/wildlife around you
- ➢ Live more sustainably/reduce pollution
- ➢ Ask to connect

Eleven

Angelic Helper's

"He will command His angels concerning you to guard you in all your ways."
- Psalm 91:11

The role of our guardian angel/s is to light, guard, rule, and guide. Our guardian angels are not looking for attention. They draw us into God's praises and presence, bringing our gaze towards the Holy Divine Source.

I never recommend praying to angels, or any other spirits than to the Holy Spirit directly. There are still ways to communicate with, commune with, and acknowledge our Divine helpers.

<u>**Connect to your guardian angel.**</u>

You can call on as many angels as you wish and as often as you desire. They love to come to your aid!

You can call on an archangel or your guardian angel with a simple prayer. Your sincere desire to connect is all that is required. For example, you can say, "Thank you, Archangel Michael, for helping me through this scary situation. I welcome your protection and guidance."

It is important to be clear that you're inviting in *only* the guides of the highest truth and compassion. It is important to immerse yourself into the Divine Spirit before you do any metaphysical work. If you do this, you can trust that no lower-vibration beings will easily come through. When you use an archangel's name, you are clear about who you're connecting to.

Here's a prayer to say when you want guidance from any angel or spirit guide:

Thank you, Holy Divine and guides of the highest truth and compassion, for revealing to me what I need to know.

Your prayers are intentions to receive support. I like to begin these prayers with the words "thank you" because they remind me that guidance is already on the way.

Remember that all spirit guides, including angels, intervene in your life only when you ask for their help. You can exercise your free will to determine whether you will receive spiritual guidance —and whether you will follow it.

Meditate to meet your guardian angel.

To start communicating with angelic guides is to introduce yourself to your guardian angel.

Get comfortable in a quiet space, close your eyes, and begin breathing long and deep.

Using your inner self, send out the request to your guardian angel that you welcome them to reveal their name to you.

Then begin any type of relaxation meditation that you use to get calm, centered and connected to the Divine flow of energy. Take as long as you like. You may hear your guardian angel's name as an intuitive thought or an audible sound, or you may be guided to write in your journal.

If you don't receive the name in your meditation, you can trust that it's coming. Don't be surprised if hours later a name comes through in some unexpected way!

Your guardian angel will share their name in an unmissable way, so pay attention and trust your intuition. Don't question the name you receive, even if it sounds strange to you. Your guardian angel has been patiently waiting for your invitation! Expect miracles.

"Then the devil left him, and behold, angels came and were ministering to him."
Matthew 4:11

Twelve

Altar's

"Wherever an altar is found, there civilization exists."
– Joseph de Maistre

An altar is a raised area where people can honor God with offerings. It is prominent in the Bible as "God's table," a sacred place for sacrifices and gifts offered up to God.

An altar is a sacred space, a spiritual focal point and a reflection of your inner magick.

Alters can be set up anywhere that you'd like to designate as a sacred space. Some people have one set up altars in their gardens. You can set as many up as you'd like.

Making a Basic Altar

Gather supplies: If you placing your altar on an existing surface, like a table or dresser, find a piece of cloth that will define the space the altar will take up. Gather up a cup of water, a stone, a candle, and a feather.

Choose a location: This should be in a spot that is convenient, yet out of the way enough that you won't mind it being there long-term.

Identify which direction is East: This is where the sun rises from in the morning. If you are unsure, or want to be very accurate, you can use a compass.

Place the items on your altar in a sacred way: Take a deep breath and bring to focus your intention for creating this sacred space.

Place your small table or arrange your altar cloth in the place you have chosen.

Place the feather on the Eastern side of your altar, and welcome the spirits of the East: the air, intellect, gratitude for breath, intuition, etc. Your feather represents the element air.

Place your candle on the Southern edge of your altar, light it, and welcome in the spirits of the South: fire, passion, transformation, inspiration. Your candle represents the element fire.

Place your cup of water on the Western side of your altar, welcoming the spirits of the West: water, emotion, flexibility, love. Your cup of water represents the element water.

Place your stone on the Northern side of your altar and welcome the spirits of the North: the earth, nourishment, stability, grounding. Your stone represents the element earth.

Give thanks: Take a few deep breaths and smile in appreciation at the beauty you have created. Recognize the wholeness that is represented in those four simple items on your altar.

Give thanks to the spirits of each of the directions that you called and invite them to leave if they must or to stay if they wish.

That outlines a very simple, dare I say elegant, altar design for any kind of use you may want. You can add items that speak to you or include gemstones or herbs that amplify the energies of each of the elements. You can even find images that represent the directions or elements and place them in the various corners of your altar. The magick here lies in making this your own sacred space. [3]

[3] https://wemoon.ws/blogs/magickal-arts/understanding-altars-what-is-an-altar-and-how-to-bring-altar-magick-into-my-life

Thirteen

Casting a Circle

The circle acts as a portal to the realm of spirits and deities, as a protection from evil forces, and as a tool to put you in the right state of mind.

How to Cast a Circle

As you practice and grow the way you practice spirituality will change and flourish. Here is a simple way to cast a circle.

Make sure you have everything gathered you would like to use within your work/circle. Candles, journal, lighter, herbs, oils, crystals, flowers, etc.

Find a safe place to cast your circle. - The ideal place is somewhere you'll feel comforted and at ease. Interruption in the middle of a work is frustrating.

Purify the place where you will cast your circle. - First, cleanse your location physically by tidying up the spot and making things orderly. If you're outdoors, clear the area of branches, leaves, and rocks. Next, cleanse the area spiritually. Meditating, use your hands (or a wand, staff, or broom if your practice involves these items) and push negative energy from the spot. You can also visualize the Divine Spirit flowing through and cleansing everything.

You could also try using a cleansing agent like witch hazel, sage, patchouli, or lavender to cleanse the area - a couple of drops in each corner of the room and round the perimeter of the circle should be sufficient.

Physically determine the bounds of your circle. – Do this by drawing a circle on the floor, sprinkling salt water in a circle, consider using the elements of nature to create your circle. Create a circle of rocks or other natural elements if it seems appropriate to your ritual or practice.

You can also visualize and use pure energy to create a circle.

Place all the objects you will be using in your ritual inside the circle. – Once you start practicing, you're going to want to stay in the circle and not break the connection until your ritual is completed. If you start and you've forgotten a particular candle or totem that's important to you, getting up and hitting "pause" isn't an option. Gather everything you'll need to begin your ritual and start preparing for your ritual.

If you're going to offer something to a spirit, remember to include that and everything you'll need to prepare it. Bring a surface to set them on, like a box or crate with a small black tablecloth.

Complete the circle. - Place candles or other items (I often like to use an element that matches each cardinal point- East -Air, South - Fire, West - Water, or North - Earth, at each cardinal direction. Do not light them yet.

Salt, a stone, or a green candle could represent Earth. Incense, broken glass, or a yellow candle could stand in for Air. Water in any container is a fine representation of water, or a blue candle for Water. A red candle does nicely for Fire.

Bless the circle. - How you choose to use your circle once its cast is largely up to you, your practice, and your goals. In general, though, you'll want to start by blessing the space and clearing it of negative energy, beginning the invocation of Divine Spirit or other spirit you're seeking to commune with. Do what feels natural.

If you must leave the circle before you are done, cut a doorway. Envision a doorway being cut from the edge of the circle, up, to the side, then down again. Reclose the circle once you're back in.

State the purpose of the circle. - If you're looking to ask the Divine for guidance, an answer, to deepen your own connection with the Spiritual or any other work. "O Circle of Power, create a meeting place of love and joy and truth; a shield against all wickedness and evil; a boundary between men and the realms of the Mighty Ones; a rampart and protection that shall preserve and contain the power that we shall raise within."

Invoke the elements and spirits you wish to work with.

Call them to the objects that represent them. Take each of the objects that represent the elements around your circle, filling it with the power of each of them. For example, I always start with East when I call on the Divine Helpers/Angels. As I light my candle or place the object, I've chosen to represent Air/East (or both) in my circle I first acknowledge East/Air, often visualizing air moving then ask the East to assist me within my circle with Divine intent then move on to the next element/direction until the circle is complete. Once I have gone through each Cardinal Direction, I then ask the Holy/Divine Spirit to assist, seal, protect, and guide me within the Circle.

Meditate for a while now.

Meditation or astral projection might be the main act, or it serves just to shift your consciousness.

Complete your ritual. – Close the circle when you're done: pay respect to whatever spirits you invited, thank the Divine, and elements before you remove their representative objects/blow out candles, and use your wand/hand/mind to release the Circle.

Don't forget to write about any experiences or lack you had during your Circle.

Fourteen

Sun & Moon **Magick**

*"His mercies never fail.
They are new every
morning."*
Lamentations 3:22-23

Sun Magick

The sun has phases which can be used with your Magickal endeavors to add an extra boost energy. Each phase of the Sun works best with specific intentions.

Sunrise – New beginnings, guidance to the right path, making changes, rejuvenation of hope and trust, a reclamation of joy, recovery of good health, and physical energy.

Morning – Growth, expansion,

drawing positivity, such as love, friendships, forgiveness, healing, overcoming, money/success. Great for courage.

Noon – Best time to charge your tools (altar, crystals, etc.). The Sun is the strongest and most powerful. Focus your intentions. love, finance, justice, and protection. This energy is unequalled when it comes to charging crystals and metal ritual tools. Excellent time for health magick, extra burst of will/energy, strength, and personal energy, study, knowledge retention, extreme illumination, and magnification.

Afternoon – A Versatile Sun phase. Clarity, reflection, professional matters, and focus.
Manage projects that need clarity and resolution, communications, and all interactions with other people. Rituals concerning new ideas, adventures, and travel are successful, use wisdom,

tenacity, and the skills to cut through deceit. A good time to balance the checkbook.

Sunset – Break bad habits, alleviate depression, and stress. Find answers, simplify, tie up loose ends, the perfect atmosphere for work that involves dieting, end bad habits, eradicate stress, confusion, and poor health. Uncover deception, practice divinatory skills and psychic activity.

Sun Water

Sun water: Sun water is water that has been charged by the energy of the Sun. Put Water into a jar, bowl, or other receptacle of your choice, place the water in the Sunlight to absorb the Sun's powerful energy.
You can use different phases of the Sun for more specific intentions or leave it out from Sunrise to Sunset for powerful results.

Uses: Place this water on your altar, clean magickal tools with it before rituals, and use it to wash your hands, face, or hair, make a spray to cleanse negative energies.

Moon Magick

Here is the overview of the 8 phases of the Moon and how you can use the energies of each of them to enhance the power of your rituals, spells and potions.

Phases of the Moon and How to Use Them

New Moon Magick– The New Moon is the first phase of the lunar cycle, starting when the Moon reappears in the night sky after 2-3 days of absence known as the 'Dark Moon'. It is a period of new beginnings; therefore, ideal for setting intentions and planting seeds for the future. Allow your imagination to run free and dream a new reality into being. This time is perfect for taking those initial steps towards manifesting your desires.

Waxing Crescent Moon Magick - The Waxing Crescent Moon is the phase of the lunar cycle in which the Moon grows. Energies are highly magnetic, making it a good time to perform 'constructive' magick - calling in what you want from life and reality, whether those are projects, plans or emotional states and behaviors, like more self-love, compassion, a positive attitude, courage, etc. The energy of the Waxing Crescent is all about going within and 'pulling' out what you want more of before you start thinking and envisioning what you want to bring forth from the external world.

First Quarter Moon Magick – While the New Moon is about going within and bringing out, the First Quarter Moon is all about attraction from the external world. It is the optimal time for performing magick that aims to draw things in, whether it is a person (partner, friend, client) or success, money, etc. Also, this is a very conducive time to call back lost objects.

Waxing Gibbous Moon Magick – Still in the 'constructive' magick phase, the energies of the Waxing Gibbous Moon are great for giving that extra push to something you've been working on but may have been stagnating. If you are struggling with lack of motivation to finish a project or stick to a routine, make use of these energies to give you a push and help you overcome temptations and resistance.

Full Moon Magick – The phase of the Full Moon is the most powerful of the cycle, and therefore the most conducive to addressing major issues or challenges you may be facing. Focus your spells and rituals on things that are of the utmost importance to your life. Also, this time is great for magick and meditations revolving around psychic development, spirituality and divination.

Waning Gibbous Moon Magick – After the Full Moon, we enter the waning phase in which energies are conducive to repelling, banishing, and destroying that which is unwanted. Use this phase to perform spells and rituals aimed at minor banishing's and cleansings, whether in physical terms or bringing closure to something that hasn't been working for a while. To realize what those are, this is a wonderful time for introspection and gaining clarity on what is no longer in alignment with your goals.

Third Quarter Moon Magick - If you've encountered an obstacle or 'bump in the road' as you work towards your goals, this is the perfect time to overcome it. Use spells that aim to boost you over hurdles that may tempt you to give up. The same goes for any transitions that you might be in midst of - make the best of these energies to smooth out any wrinkles and make the process flow with more ease.

Waning Crescent Moon Magick - Closer to the Dark Moon phase, energies are more suitable for performing serious banishing's, getting rid of anything that has been absorbing joy from your life and draining your energy. If there's anything you wish to just cut out from your life, work with the energies of this period to do so.

<u>Ritual</u>

A ritual could be as simple as lighting a candle, or as in-depth as a long, fully scripted group extravaganza. Your ritual may include howling at the full Moon or sitting in contemplative silence.

You may envision gathering with friends around a fire or taking a solitary Moon bath. To turn any action into a ritual, use your power of intention setting and make that intention reflect out bright as the stars on a dark New Moon night.[4]

Moon Water

The making of moon water is traditionally undertaken during a waxing or full moon, when the lunar cycle is at its fullest, in support of abundance and creation. If you'd like, you can make moon water during other lunar phases and manifest the respective energies.

A new moon will help inspire spaciousness and rest. A waning moon will help you release or shed unwanted energy. Beware making moon water during an eclipse, which initiates a turbulent vibe.

---

[4] https://www.centreofexcellence.com/moon-magic-impact-lunar-cycle-magical-activities/

Focus on your intention and keep it in mind throughout the process, visualizing what you desire without distracting yourself with notions of how it will happen. Simply allow yourself to feel as though what you want to experience in your life is already taking place.

Using Moon Water

Drinking – Sip moon water, or mix it into a drink of your choice, taking in the energy and allowing it to empower you.

Watering Plants – Moon water can be shared with your houseplants, garden beds, or trees.

Cleansing – Clean sacred spaces, use a cloth or sponge in the moon water, and wipe the surface.
Use moon water in a spritz bottle and mist any space where you'd like to invite a serene and supportive atmosphere. If desired, add essential oil to the water.

Bathing – Moon water can make an exquisite addition to your skincare routine or bathing ritual, imbuing your body with the gentle energy of the moon.
Washing your face with the water is an option.
Moon water in your bathwater not only cleanses your physical body but allows the moon's vibes to envelop you, promoting relaxation, rejuvenation, and connection to your intentions.

Fifteen

"Trees exhale for us so that we can inhale them to stay alive. Can we ever forget that? Let us love trees with every breath we take until we perish."

- Munia Khan

Herb's, Plant's, & Tree's

Through the ages people have turned to nature and flora not only for food and medicines, but also as a means of connecting with the spiritual realm.

Several plants that acted as a bridge to the supernatural are part of the extensive collection of herbs within the <u>Robison Herb Garden</u>, where they reside in the <u>Herbs of the Ancients</u>, <u>Herbs</u>

in <u>Literature</u>, and <u>Medicinal Herbs</u>.

Many of these plants demand our respect, not because they open a pathway to the supernatural, but because they can make us sick or worse.

<u>**Here is a list of plants with a history.**</u>

Vervain
Verbena officinalis also known as the Enchanter's herb, has a long association with magickal and spiritual practices going back in time to the ancient Egyptians, Greeks, and Romans, as well as the Celtic Druids. Vervain's primary role was to protect believers against evil spells or negative energy and to purify sacred places, such as altars, ceremonial implements, temples, and private dwellings.

Poppy (*Papaver somniferum*)
In Greek mythology, Demeter was

worshipped as the goddess of agriculture, the seasons, and the harvest, and she instructed mortals in how to cultivate wheat and barley. The well-known story of Demeter and her daughter Persephone entails the abduction of Persephone by Hades, the Greek god of the Underworld. Demeter was given the poppy plant by the god Morpheus to ease her grief and suffering. Demeter and her daughter Persephone were also at the center of an ancient cult known as the Eleusinian Mysteries. Followers believed the two goddesses possessed medical knowledge and skills for treating illnesses of women and children.

Deadly Nightshade (*Atropa belladonna*)
A highly poisonous plant, Deadly Nightshade's name comes from the Greek mythological character Atropos, one of the three fates whose role was to cut the thread of human life. The plant was used in ancient times as an effective poison, but also in anesthesia preparations. Atropine, an alkaloid derived from the plant, continues to be used in surgery to control salivation and to regulate the

heart rate. Deadly Nightshade, also known as Belladonna, was used in witchcraft as a flying ointment. When the plant was soaked in fat then applied externally it induced the sensation of flying or astral projection, due to its hallucinogenic effects.

Henbane (*Hyoscyamus niger*)
One of the ingredients used in anesthesia by the ancient Egyptians, Greeks, and Romans, Henbane's leaves are a source of hyoscyamine, atropine, hyoscine, and scopolamine, chemicals that act on the central nervous system. In the Middle Ages, the plant was associated with witchcraft, as it was one of the ingredients used to make flying ointment. Henbane is not to be trifled with—it can cause death due to respiratory and heart failure if ingested.

Aconite, Monkshood (*Aconitum nepellus*)
In Greek mythology, Aconite was associated with the goddess Hekate and was formed from the caustic saliva of the three headed monster dog, Cerberus, who guarded the gates of hell. It was listed as

one of the ingredients in witches' flying ointments, but due to its lethal toxicity, this application is in question. It is one of the most poisonous plants of the Old World and was used to poison wolves, as well as human foes.

Lady's Mantle (*Alchemilla mollis*; *Alchemilla xanthochlora*)
During the Middle Ages people thought that the glassy beads of liquid that form overnight on *Alchemilla's* pleated leaves was imbued with a magickal essence that was used to create the Philosopher's Stone. Alchemists believed the Stone could transform base metals into gold, cure all diseases, and prolong life. The name *Alchemilla* originates with the Arabic word for chemistry, *al-kimiya'* and translates to "the little alchemical one".

More Plants A-Z

Aloe - Protection and luck. Place on the grave of a loved one to promote peaceful energy. Thought to relieve loneliness and assist with success. Hang in the home to attract luck and protection for those who live there. Grow in the home to provide protection from household accidents. Burn on the night of a full moon to bring a new lover by the new moon. Also Called: Burn Plant, Medicine Plant

Apple – Garden magick, love, healing, and wisdom, also vanity, marriage, and beauty. Associated Mabon and Samhain. Element water.

Ash – Spells relating to the sea, protection, and luck. Make your Yule log from ash and burn to bring prosperity. Yggdrasil was an Ash tree. Element water.

Basil – Also called witches' herb. Use in spells for Love, exorcism, wealth, sympathy, and protection. Associated with Imbolc. Aids astral projection. Element Fire.

Bay Leaf (&Laurel) – Protection, success, purification, strength, wisdom, and healing, also increases psychic powers. Element Fire.

Beech – Happiness, inspiration, and divination. Represents the Green Man. Element Air.

Belladonna – Also Called: Deadly Nightshade. Toxic. Use for forgetting past loves. Protection, beauty, and original flying ointments. Adds energy to rituals. Element Water.

Birch – Protection, exorcism, and purification. Dispels lightning, infertility, and the evil eye. Associated with Yule. Element Water.

Black Pepper – Banishing negativity, exorcism, and offers protection and help with inner strength. Element Fire

Blackthorn – Exorcisms, warding off negative spirits and general protection.

Associated with Samhain. Element Earth.

Blueberry - Protection of children, keeps evil out, and strengthens the aura. Associated with the Great Spirit. Element Water.

Carnation - Protection, strength, healing, enhancing magickal powers, and achieving balance. Element Fire.

Catnip - Also called Nepeta. Use when working with animals. Draws love, luck, and happiness, also used in beauty magick. Associated with Bast. Element Water.

Cedarwood - Luck, strength, and power. Helps increase money and protection. Also healing. Associated with Mabon. Element Earth.

Celandine - Cures depression, treats piles, improves circulation. Brings about Joy and happiness. Solar Magick. Element Fire.

Chamomile - Love, sleep, protection, and purification, also reduce stress. Use for meditation work and to attract money. Solar Magick. Element Water.

Chickweed - Also called Witches Grass. Use in moon spells. Also good for animal magick, relationships, love, and fertility. Element Water.

Chili - Fidelity, love, and passion. Also, hex breaking. Element Fire.

Cinnamon – Also known as Sweet Wood. Use for Solar magick. Meditation and astral projection. Increases spirituality, success, healing, protection, power, luck, strength, and prosperity. Element Fire.

Clover, Red - Also called Trefoil. used in any spells relating to marriage, love, lust, and fidelity. Aids success and money. Element Air.

Clove - Use to protect, banish negative forces, and divination. Also helps with any teeth spells. Aids money and draws love. Element Fire.

Coriander – Love, lust, and health. Used as an aphrodisiac and to heal migraines. Brings peace and protection to the home. Element Fire.

Cornflower – Used primarily as an Ink for your Book of Shadows. It is the patron herb of herbalists. Use in rituals to give honor to the Mother of all nature, also connected to Rainbow and Crystal children. Element Earth.

Cumin – Fidelity, protection, and exorcism. Also used in love spells and food which can also promote fidelity. Element Earth

Cypress – Associated with death and mourning; stimulates healing and helps overcome the pain of loss. Other properties include self-esteem, protection, love, and banishing nightmares. Element Earth.

Dandelion Leaf - Used to summon spirits, make wishes on, healing, purification and defeating negativity. Element Air.

Dandelion Root - Magickal uses include divination, wishes and calling spirits. It also enhances dreams and works well in astral projection. Element Air.

Echinacea - Adds a boost to clairvoyant and psychic abilities. Adds powerful strength to spells used in money drawing magick, fertility and abundance and provides the user with protective power. Element Earth.

Elder Tree - Sleep, releasing enchantments, protection against negativity, banishing.

Elderflower and **Berry** - Peace, protection, and healing, plus aids in exorcisms. Element Water.

Elm - Energizes the mind and balances the heart. Aids love spells and offers protection from lightning. Element Water.

Evening Primrose - Ideal for moon magick. Also use in love charms and to attract fae. Element Water.

Frankincense Resin - Use in solar magick. Associated with Beltane, Lammas, and Yule. Use in rituals and magick associated with self-control, spirituality, and protection. Also regulates emotions and helps depression. Element Earth

Garlic - Magickal uses include speed, health, and endurance, also protection, exorcism, and purification. Use also to promote your inner strength. Element Fire.

Ginger - Increases magick power. Success, love, money, and power. Element Fire.

Ginseng - Promotes love, beauty, healing, and lust. Element Fire.

Hawthorn Wood- Associated with Beltane. Magickal uses include chastity, fertility, fairy magick, fishing magick, and rebirth. Success in career, work, and employment. Use it to work with the fae. Used in weddings and handfasting's to increase fertility. Element Water. Hawthorne Berries aid chastity. Hope, protection, and happiness. Element Fire.

Hibiscus - Attracting love and lust. Use in divination. Associated with lunar magick. Element Water.

Holly Hock - Protecting, all Fairy magick, abundance, personal growth and aids passing. Related to Lammas. Element Earth.

Ivy - Protection, healing, and fertility. Use for love and hang at handfasting's. Element Fire.

Jasmine - The herb of attraction. Helps prophetic dreaming, money, and love. Element Water.

Juniper - See Cedar berries.

Lavender - Magickal uses include healing, sleep, and peace. It also promotes chastity and love. Increases longevity of life, tranquility, and happiness. Element Air.

Lemon Grass - Psychic cleansing and opening. Use in lust potions and when using Dragon Magick. Element Air.

Lilac - Wisdom, memory, good luck, and spiritual aid. Element Water.

Mandrake - Spell strengthener. Use for protection, happiness, and wealth. It aids money multiplying. Element Earth.

Marigold - See Calendula.

Marjoram - Use for cleansing, purification, and dispelling negativity. Also aids grief and sadness. Element Air.

Mint – Promotes energy, communication and vitality, protection and draws custom. Element Air.

Mistletoe – Also called Witches Broom. Used for fertility, creativity, and protection from negative spells and magick. Hang at handfasting to kiss beneath and promote peace. Element Air.

Mugwort – Use for strength, protection, and healing. Mugwort amplifies magick. Aids astral projection, and psychic power.   Element Earth.

Mullein – Represents the crossroads. Offers protection from nightmares and hexing. Attracts love and keeps evil energies and spirits at bay. Element Fire.

Mustard Seed – Courage, faith, and endurance. It is a good luck amulet. Aids mental power and offers protection. Element Fire.

Myrrh – Spiritual, meditation, and healing. Supports youthfulness and protection. Luck and peace. Element Earth.

Nettle – Uses include dispelling darkness & fear, and curse breaking. Healing and protection and increase lust in partners. Renewal. Element Fire.

Nutmeg – Magickal uses include attracting money/prosperity, and luck. Use for fortune telling and when you need favorable decisions. Element Fire.

Oak – Connected to Litha and the most sacred of all trees. Oak supports success, good luck, and healing. Stability and potency and attracts money. Element Water.

Orange Peel and Flower – Attracts abundance, luck. Love and happiness strengthens divination. Element Fire.

Oregano – Aids astral projection, health, and vitality. Increase joy and justice and protects against evil. Use at Handfasting's. Element Air.

Parsley – Use this herb to help with contacting the dead. Increases strength, vitality and passion. It is uplifting and helps spiritual growth. Element Air.

Passionflower – Attracts friendship and passion. Calming, peace and instills passion into stale relationships. Good for house blessings too. Element Water.

Peppermint – Use for headaches and other forms of healing. Increases sleep and love. Use for increasing psychic power and divination. Element Air.

Pine/Needles – Prosperity and success. Protection, purification, and divination. Throw in the fire to dispel negativity. Use in house and business blessings. Element Fire.

Poppy Seeds – Pleasure, love, and luck. Aids sleep and insomnia. Use in astral projection and flying magick. Increases fertility and happiness. Element Water.

Pumpkin Seed – Use in lunar magick to honor the moon. Also healing and increases divination. Element Fire.

Raspberry Leaf – Used for healing, protection, love. Raspberry leaf is not to ingested (ate) by pregnant women until due date, induces labor. Helps to reduce the pain involved in childbirth. Supports sleep, dreams, and love. Element Water.

Red Clover – Aids success, love, and money. Increases fidelity. Use in exorcism. Element Air.

Rose – Use for divination, increased psychic power, love, lust, and healing. Helps strengthen close friendships. Place around sprains and bruises to help them heal faster. Element Water.

Rose Hips – Used in healing spells or to bring good luck and invoking good spirits. Aids stronger love. Element Water.

Rosemary - Use in healing poppets and love/lust spells. Improves memory. Increases sleep, mental power, and protection. Burn to help purification and removing negativity. Associated with faery magick. Element Fire.

Sage - Used for self-purification and cleansing. Helps grief and loss. Healing and protection, also increases wisdom. Element Air.

Sandalwood - Burn during protection, healing, and exorcism spells. Aids luck and success, meditation, and divination. Raises a high spiritual vibration. Element Water.

Sea Salt - Use to cleanse crystals and tools. For purification, grounding, and protection. Supports ritual work. Absorbs negativity and banishes evil. Element Earth and Water.

St. John's Wort - Worn to prevent colds and fevers. Induces prophetic and romantic dreams. Protects against hexes and black witchcraft. Increases happiness. Use in Solar Magick. Element Fire.

Star Anise - Consecration, purification, and happiness. Use for curse breaking or increasing luck. Burn to increase psychic awareness. Element Fire.

Strawberry Leaf - Attracts success, good fortune, and favorable circumstances. Increases love and aids pregnancy. Element Water.

Sunflower - Energy, protection, and power. Aids wisdom and brings about wishes. Use in fertility magick. Element Fire.

Tea Leaves - Use for courage or strength. In tea for increasing lust. Burn leaves to ensure future riches. Element Air.

Thistle - or Holy Thistle. Purification, protection against negativity and evil, hex breaking and aids vitality. Wear or keep with you for strength and protection. Element Earth.

Thyme - Attracts loyalty, affection, and love. Increases good luck and psychic power. Drink in tea to aid sleep. Element Air.

Valerian - Also called Graveyard dust. Helps sleep, calming and a sedative. Quietens emotions. Supports protection and love. Element Water.

White Willow Bark - Use in lunar magick. Reduces negativity and removes evil forces and hexes. Use in healing spells. (Aspirin) Element Water. (over-use can cause vision issues)

Willow - Used for lunar magick, drawing, or strengthening love, healing, and overcoming sadness. Element Water.

Wormwood – Used to remove anger, stop war, inhibit violent acts, and for protection. Use in clairvoyance, to summon spirits, or to enhance divinatory abilities. Element Earth.

Yarrow – Healing, calming and increases love. Used in handfasting and weddings. Increases psychic power and divination. Gives courage when needed. Element Air.

Sixteen

*"In a crystal we have clear evidence of
the existence of a formative life principle,
and though we cannot understand the
life of a crystal,
it is nonetheless a living being."*
– *Nikola Tesla*

Crystals

Many ancient cultures — including ones
in Egypt, Greece, and China — believed
that crystals have healing properties.
Some people claim that crystals promote
the flow of good energy and help rid your
body and mind of negative energy for
physical and emotional benefits. In some
belief systems, practitioners place
gemstones on certain areas of the body to
promote healing.

Gems are used as part of spiritual practices and can aid in meditation, spells, and potions. Incorporate gems into rituals to restore energy fields, gain peace, and promote love and safety.

Crystals A-Z

Agate - Passion and creativity to relaxing stillness. There is one thing that all Agate stones have in common, however. They're all master's at lifting your spirits.

- **Chakra:** All
- **Zodiac sign:** Gemini
- **Best for:** Clarity, Calming Energy, Uplifting Energy

Alabaster - Commonly referred to as the 'Drawing Stone', Magnetically pull things you need towards you. Alabaster is a great stone to use in intention-setting or manifestation practices. Treat it like your personal prosperity magnet. Great at soothing tension and relaxing your muscles after a long day.

- **Chakra:** Root, Sacral
- **Zodiac sign:** Aries
- **Best for:** Manifestation, Intentions, Prosperity

Amazonite - Known as the 'Stone of Hope', Amazonite brings peace and love to all decisions. Enables you to be free and playful, knowing that you are protected at the highest possible level. Maintain optimism, consciously choose positive and joy-bringing thoughts rather than negative ones. Rejuvenating energy helps you find peace within. Stimulates both the heart and throat chakras, helping you articulate yourself clearly and with love.

- **Chakra:** Heart, Throat

- **Zodiac sign:** Virgo
- **Best for:** Hope, Communication, Trust, Emotional Healing

Amethyst - Sleep, dreams, and all things spiritual, tranquil vibes, facilitating a deep and unparalleled relaxation. Relieves anxiety or insomnia. Connecting with the spiritual realm. Activating the higher chakras, including the etheric chakra that sits above your physical body, Amethyst acts as a doorway between the physical realms and the spiritual realms. It can be used to open a dialogue with spirit guides as well as to enhance lucid dreaming or astral projection.

- **Chakra:** Third Eye, Crown, Etheric
- **Zodiac sign:** Virgo, Sagittarius, Capricorn, Aquarius, Pisces
- **Best for:** Sleep, Tranquility, Clairvoyance

Angelite - A spiritual powerhouse, all things metaphysical. Enhance lucid dreaming, and astral projection. A high-frequency stone, Unveils psychic powers. Uncovers new senses, abilities, and perceptions.

- **Chakra:** Throat, Third Eye, Crown
- **Zodiac sign:** Aquarius
- **Best for:** Lucid Dreaming, Psychic Abilities, Clairvoyance, Astral Projection

Antigorite - Aid longevity, detoxifying the blood and body. Antigorite generally works on the lower chakras, helping to stabilize your energy and anchor you in the present moment. It can also stimulate the rise of kundalini energy through your energetic centers.

- **Chakra:** Root, Solar Plexus
- **Zodiac sign:** Gemini
- **Best for:** Emotional Balance, Longevity, Grounding

Apatite – Apatite is the name given to a family of stones that raise your energy and boost your connection with the spiritual realm. Provides an abundance of positive energy. They're great stones to work with if you've been feeling low recently. Apatite is a sure-fire way to get you back into a high-vibe spirit.

- **Chakra:** Solar Plexus, Heart, Throat, Third Eye
- **Zodiac sign:** Gemini, Capricorn, Pisces
- **Best for:** Positive Energy, Vertical Vision, Meditation

Aquamarine – Soothing worries and anxious thoughts, keeps your energy centered. Can be used to keep seasickness or travel sickness. Soothing vibes are like a refreshing splash of water on a hot summer's day. Stimulating the throat chakra, helps with articulating your thoughts, emotions, and ideas too. Aquamarine helps you speak with clarity and precision.

- **Chakra:** Heart, Throat

- **Zodiac sign:** Aries, Gemini, Pisces
- **Best for:** Calming Energy, Stress-Relief, Communication, Seasickness

Azurite - Azurite is the stone of insight. Its energy cleanses and strengthens your emotional body-it inspires you to let go of worries and nagging negative thoughts that linger in the back of your consciousness. Gives you the ability to understand the root of your fears and phobias, so you can more easily let them go. Overcome behavioral patterns that stem from insecurity and lack of self-worth, teaching you how to love and accept yourself for who you are.

- **Chakra:** Third eye
- **Zodiac sign:** Taurus, Aquarius, Sagittarius
- **Best for:** Insight, Intuition, Intellect

Barite – Let go of the things in your life that do not serve you any longer. Welcome change in your life, and transition smoothly in all your new endeavors. Release of stagnant energy and negative emotions and replaces them with unconditional love. Dream recall and memory retention. Open your mind to receiving the wisdom of the Universe.

- **Chakra:** Third eye, Crown
- **Zodiac sign:** Aquarius
- **Best for:** Change, Release, Dream Recall

Beryl – Release unhealthy thought patterns and emotional baggage. Bravery and determination. Instills a sense of relaxation and peace. Balances empathy with logic and allows you to make the most informed and accurate decisions. Motivation and drive to act where necessary.

- **Chakra:** All
- **Zodiac sign:** Scorpio, Sagittarius, Pisces

- **Best for:** Emotional Healing, Relaxation, Balance

Black Kyanite – Known as the revival stone. It has a high vibration, which translates into the ability to remove blockages quickly, and it is one of the few black stones that cannot store negative energies. Effective for opening the base chakra, it can be used to balance the entire chakra system, keeping life force flowing harmoniously. Cleanse and amplify other crystals.

- **Chakra:** Root
- **Zodiac sign:** Taurus, Libra, Aries
- **Best for:** Cleansing, Removing Blockages, Chakra Harmonization

Black Obsidian – Protective stone. Ground and root to mother earth, ensuring your inner strength is always activated. Security and stability in any situation. Encourages introspection – it was used in scrying mirrors for centuries. This deep soul cleanser promotes self-reflection and enables you to pinpoint your own bad habits; negative thoughts, beliefs, or subconscious actions; and root causes of issues. Empowers you to overcome your flaws one at a time.

- **Chakra:** Root
- **Zodiac sign:** Sagittarius, Scorpio
- **Best for:** Protection, Grounding Energy, Self-Reflection

Black Onyx – Heals emotional and mental issues, channeling them into a greater purpose. Acknowledge your inner-being, accept, and be present without feeling drained or burdened.

- **Chakra:** Root
- **Zodiac sign:** Leo, Capricorn

- **Best for:** Positive Energy, Channeling, Emotional Healing

Bloodstone – Maintain your energetic system, clearing any sluggish or negative energy from your environment. Purifying stone, banishing negativity with ease, and working to protect your energy field. Grounding yourself and focus, and stabilizing energy.

- **Chakra:** Root
- **Zodiac sign:** Pisces, Aries, Libra
- **Best for:** Purification, Protection, Stability

Blue Apatite - Come to terms with your emotions. Personal growth helps you progress. Let go of emotions that are no longer serving you. Ambition and motivation. Express your authentic self honestly to the world.

- **Chakra:** Third eye
- **Zodiac sign:** Gemini
- **Best for:** Progress, Ambition, Honesty

Blue Aventurine – Confidence and calmness. Inspiration that can help you overcome obstacles in your path such as writer's block or other challenges. Promotes confidence in public speaking and in communicating effectively with anyone on your journey. Heightens awareness of the angelic realm.

- **Chakra:** Throat
- **Zodiac sign:** Aquarius, Libra
- **Best for:** Confidence, Communication, Calmness

Blue Calcite – Sharpens intuition and psychic insight. Connects you to your higher self and to your subconscious mind. Process and transmute negative energies from your past lives as well as from currently. Raise your vibration and make progress on your path. Spiritual growth and development that enhances your ability to communicate and overcome social anxiety.

- **Chakra:** Throat

- **Zodiac sign:** Cancer
- **Best for:** Social Anxiety, Spiritual Growth, Communication

Blue Jade – Removes the tendency to be overwhelmed and stressed, encourages rational thought and intelligence. Known as a dream stone, opens you up to receiving important messages from the universe in your dreams. Dream recall and dream interpretation. Especially useful when faced with self-inflicted barriers to success.

- **Chakra:** Throat, third eye
- **Zodiac sign:** Taurus
- **Best for:** Rational Thought, Dreaming, Insight

Blue Sandstone – New beginnings and success. Fuel your ambition or new ventures, manifest your intentions. Balances your chakras to facilitate self-acceptance, relieve stress, help you speak your truth freely, and increase focus. Protection stone that deflects negative energy and shields your auric field from unwanted vibrations. Instills positive energy, boosts your mood, and uplifts your spirit.

- **Chakra:** Throat, third eye
- **Zodiac sign:** Sagittarius
- **Best for:** New Beginnings, Success, Ambition

Calcite – Discern which pieces of information are the most important. Keep your energy calm and collected whenever you feel provoked. Study more effectively. Combats feelings of laziness and gives you bursts of energy. Eases the emotional stress that you may be feeling and replaces that feeling with peace. Stabilizing stone, increases your ability to trust others and yourself.

- **Chakra:** All
- **Zodiac sign:** Cancer
- **Best for:** Discernment, Drive, Stability

Celestite - Connects you to angelic realms. Receive information from higher beings and guardian angels. Spiritual strength, Connects you to the divine nature of everything. Entering a vortex of cosmic knowledge, Celestite could temporarily transport your awareness to a non-physical plane where everything seems to make sense, despite its complex intricacies.

- **Chakra:** Throat

- **Zodiac sign:** Libra, Gemini
- **Best for:** Spirituality, Awareness, Strength

Chrysoprase – Hope. Could assist your heart in preparing for new love and new relationships. Promotes joy, happiness, and forgiveness, confidence, and independence, taking more control over life. Alleviates mental exhaustion. Surfaces talents and gifts you possess, inspires you to use them to create the life you've always wanted.

- **Chakra:** Heart
- **Zodiac sign:** Gemini, Aquarius
- **Best for:** Hope, Forgiveness, Confidence

Citrine - Cleanse spaces of negative energies and spirits. Release tension in your emotional body and let go of anger. Overcome feelings of confusion, depression, and fear. Increases your self-worth, take criticism gracefully. Helps with relationships and attract pleasure into your life. Attunes you to vibrations of wealth and abundance, and creativity, bringing prosperity into your life.

- **Chakra:** Solar plexus, sacral
- **Zodiac sign:** Aries, Leo, Libra
- **Best for:** Wealth, Abundance, Pleasure

Clear Quartz - Mental clarity, a perfect tool for increasing quick wit, rational thinking, and focus. Dispels negative energy and supercharges the intentions set, intensifying your energy. Deepens your meditative state and quietens thoughts with its mind-stilling effects.

- **Chakra:** Crown
- **Zodiac sign:** Aries
- **Best for:** Clarity, Focus, Meditation

Diamond – Purity and love. Everlasting love, and fidelity. Stay loyal and faithful to your partner, dedicated, and devoted in your relationship. Assists a strong and healthy relationship. Enhances creative spirit and imagination, encouraging you to find new ways of looking at the same situation and allowing the inner child in you to shine.

- **Chakra:** Crown
- **Zodiac sign:** Virgo, Libra
- **Best for:** Purity, Fidelity, Creativity

Emerald – Powerful healing stone for the heart chakra. Promotes positive thinking. Inspires compassion and generosity. Open your inner empath.

- **Chakra:** Heart
- **Zodiac sign:** Taurus, Gemini
- **Best for:** Love, Hope, Compassion

Fire Agate – Guard against negative energy in your environment and from toxic energy in your body. Deflects any ill wishes that have been placed on you. Allows you to feel more energized in your pursuit of your dreams and goals. Creativity and inspiration. Break out of negative and harmful thought patterns and cycles.

- **Chakra:** Root
- **Zodiac sign:** Gemini, Capricorn
- **Best for:** Energization, Creativity, Release

Fluorite – Healing. Comes in many colors, for this reason, depending on which type of Fluorite you have, you can use it to activate all your chakras. Boosts mental clarity and clears away brain fog. Helps concentration.

- **Chakra:** All
- **Zodiac sign:** Capricorn
- **Best for:** Clarity, Focus

Garnet - Inner strength and helps find peace in the present moment. Healing, and removing negative energy in the bedroom. Masculine and feminine energies, and the divine merging of the two through the art of sex. Libido boost or a burst of passion.

- **Chakra:** Root
- **Zodiac sign:** Capricorn
- **Best for:** Passion, Sexual Energy, Courage

Green Apatite – Achieve your dreams, accomplishing them with ease. Clears doubt, fear, and confusion that you may have on your path to spiritual and personal development. Brings knowledge and truth required to manifest dreams with quicker speed and greater confidence. Connects you to nature spirits and reconnects you to the Earth's healing and nurturing energies.

- **Chakra:** Heart
- **Zodiac sign:** Taurus, Virgo

- **Best for:** Guidance, Personal Growth, Nature

Green Aventurine – "Stone of Opportunity," one of the luckiest crystals. Promotes a feeling of forgiveness and acceptance of human nature. Beneficial for all those who experience fear, anxiety, and restlessness. A positive stone, symbolizing inner peace, curbing negative energy, and promoting spiritual growth. Aligns your vibration with that of Mother Nature and encourages you to engage in personal growth.

- **Chakra:** Heart
- **Zodiac sign:** Libra
- **Best for:** Opportunity, Luck, Personal Growth

Howlite – Calmness, peace, deep reflection, and tranquility. Grow spiritually by placing you in a position of calm acceptance and quieting your spirit. Deepen your meditative state, balance, and activate your crown chakra. Promotes self-reflection, free from narcissism or negativity. Look deeply at your personal truth and gives the courage to adjust where needed. Regulate the temper and is useful in promoting better self-tolerance and acceptance.

- **Chakra:** Crown
- **Zodiac sign:** Gemini
- **Best for:** Calmness, Meditation, Self-Reflection

Iolite – Guides you towards your desires. This gemstone is like holding a magnet for success. Iolite is a light in the darkness that helps you pinpoint your purpose with precision. It helps you connect with your inner self, improve your well-being, and follow your intended life path.

- **Chakra:** Third Eye, Throat

- **Zodiac sign:** Taurus, Libra, Sagittarius
- **Best for:** Spiritual Growth, Emotional Balance

Jade – Obliterate negative energy before it has a chance to harm you. Attracts wealth and abundance, ensuring you maintain good control over your finances. Use Jade to absorb negative energy and achieve inner peace.

- **Chakra:** Heart
- **Zodiac sign:** Pisces, Virgo
- **Best for:** Self-Love, Compassion, Trust

Jasper – Awakens kundalini and removes blockages in your base chakra. Boost of motivation. Rainforest jasper is the perfect gemstone when you want to deepen the connection you have to yourself and your life. It can help instill a greater sense of self-love and compassion. Picture Jasper invites feelings of stability and balance into your life. Orbicular Jasper allows you to start afresh without doubts and uncertainty.

- **Chakra:** Root
- **Zodiac sign:** Cancer
- **Best for:** Balance, Motivation, Connection

Kunzite – Self-improvement. and forgiveness. Kunzite will help you be yourself without worrying about what others will think. It encourages you to value your own happiness more than the opinion of others. Its calming energy is enough to soothe tension and establish emotional balance.

- **Chakra:** Heart

- **Zodiac sign:** Taurus, Scorpio
- **Best for:** Peace, Relaxation, Emotional Healing

Kyanite – Connection, healing, clear thinking, and psychic ability. Aligns the chakras, brings harmony, and balance. Stone for meditation. Blue Kyanite's calming energy brings insight to your mind, while Green Kyanite connects you to nature and to your own personal development. Indigo Kyanite awakens psychic abilities like telepathy and clairvoyance, and Black Kyanite protects you from negative energy. Orange Kyanite enhances passion and creativity.

- **Chakra:** All
- **Zodiac sign:** All
- **Best for:** Insight, Personal Development, Creativity

Labradorite – Healing, relieves anxiety and stress, easing tension and encouraging you to relax and truly connect to your body. Treats disorders of the eyes, brain, and digestive system, and spiritual growth. Actively pushes you to follow your sacred calling and get in touch with your higher self. Thought to open the door between the physical realm and the spirit world.

Lapis Lazuli - Reveals inner truth and encourages the release of repressed anger and other negative emotions. Helps in building healthy social connections and relationships. Promotes empathy. Allows you to be honest with other people and maintain harmonious relationships without conflict. Stimulates psychic abilities and aids in enhancing compassion for others.

- **Chakra:** Third eye
- **Zodiac sign:** Sagittarius
- **Best for:** Truth, Relationships, Harmony

Lithium Quartz – Heart chakra stone. Achieve emotional peace. Understand the patterns and people you attract into your life, especially the relationships that end in heartache. If you find yourself repeating unhealthy cycles when it comes to friends, family or partners, Lithium Quartz can assist you in recognizing them and encourage you to make the necessary changes. Release past attachments and unhealthy expectations.

- **Chakra:** All
- **Zodiac sign:** Aquarius
- **Best for:** Peace, Relationships, Change

Malachite – New life, rebirth, energy, and growth. A stone of transformation. Assists you in much needed changes in your life. Seeing the good in the people around you, enabling you to discover the root cause for the toxicity in your life. Malachite reminds you that it's never too late to turn over a new leaf. Renews your spiritual energy and fiery passions that you have forgotten and connects you to the past while remaining grounded in the present.

- **Chakra:** Heart
- **Zodiac sign:** Scorpio, Capricorn
- **Best for:** Rebirth, Self-Discovery, Passion

Meteorite - Channel the energy of the Universe right into the palm of your hands. Balance and align the energetic fields of the body and expand consciousness beyond your physical boundaries. Introspection brings a more in-depth insight into existing problems or situations. Realize the purpose of our existence on this planet and in life. Adapt to change more readily and encourages mental growth.

- **Chakra:** Root
- **Zodiac sign:** Sagittarius
- **Best for:** Consciousness, Introspection, Purpose

Moonstone – Vitality that re-energizes. Strength and calmness, known to enhance intuition and inspire success in all avenues of your life. Wash away negative energy and rebalance the room. Brings harmony into the space it is placed and disperses any unwanted tension or stress. Encourages creativity, free expression, and fertility. Enhancing insight and vision.

- **Chakra:** Crown, third eye, heart
- **Zodiac sign:** Gemini
- **Best for:** Vitality, Intuition, Fertility

Moss Agate – Healing of emotional wounds. Inner peace when things seem too chaotic to face. It releases fear that causes emotional blocks and encourages you to apply mental concentration to the tasks at hand. Assists you in removing emotional distractions by channeling your energy towards a fun and creative goal. It reduces mood swings and brings a healthy self-esteem.

- **Chakra:** Heart

- **Zodiac sign:** Virgo
- **Best for:** Emotional Healing, Concentration, Self-Esteem

Mother of Pearl – Activates psychic abilities and clairvoyance, allowing you to see past what is right in front of you and enabling you to see into the spiritual realm. With this ability, you are able to receive important guidance and strength that you need in order to live a fruitful and meaningful life on the physical plane. Instills a sense of confidence and high self-esteem. When you do not have personal power and courage, the pearl will step in and cultivate a sense of self-confidence in you.

- **Chakra:** Crown, third eye
- **Zodiac sign:** Pisces
- **Best for:** Psychic Abilities, Guidance, Confidence

Nuummite - Its physical healing properties are astounding – it relieves pain, supports relief from stress. Relieves anxiety, bringing a soothing breath of fresh air. Brings you back to the present moment.

- **Chakra:** Root
- **Zodiac sign:** None
- **Best for:** Grounding, Stress-Relief

Obsidian - Protective stone and provides a fascinating glimpse into the subconscious workings of the mind. Other types of Obsidian such as Snowflake Obsidian or Golden Obsidian work on different areas of the body. These are more suited for ambitious people who are looking for that extra push to get stuff done.

- **Chakra:** Root, Solar Plexus, Third Eye
- **Zodiac sign:** Scorpio, Sagittarius
- **Best for:** Protection, Spiritual Growth

Onyx – Strength. This stone helps us to look inward, to confront the things we may be avoiding, and to come to terms with our weaknesses, without fear or judgment. Grow into our best selves. Its serene energy also allows us to let go of the past and move forward into the future with a sense of peace and purpose. Helps to create a protective shield around its wearer, deflecting negativity and absorbing any harmful or unwanted energies, helping sharpen our focus and keep us on the right path.

- **Chakra:** Root, Third Eye, Solar Plexus
- **Zodiac sign:** Leo
- **Best for:** Strength, Protection, Focus, Willpower, Perseverance, Determination, Self-Control

Opalite – Associated with youth and child-like wonder. Optimism and curiosity helps to go with the flow. It casts out negativity with its warm and positive energy. Puts heavy hearts at ease, especially from emotional burdens like depression. Replace feelings of anger or resentment with compassion and kindness. Brings a more positive outlook on life.

- **Chakra:** Third eye
- **Zodiac sign:** Cancer
- **Best for:** Youth, Optimism, Positivity

Pearl – Inner wisdom and connection to the cosmos. Brings messages from the divine that help along your path. A purification master, dissolve negative energies and keep you in touch with high vibes. Extraordinary healing properties. Helps with insomnia.

- **Chakra:** Crown, Heart, Third Eye
- **Zodiac sign:** Gemini
- **Best for:** Wisdom, Integrity, Purity

Peridot - Prosperity and success, abundance in all aspects of your life, not just in terms of financial independence, but also in the love and blessings you receive from the Universe. Shielding you from negativity and releasing old habits and patterns that no longer serve you. It allows you to move forward with confidence and ease. Balances and upgrades energy, boosts self-esteem.

- **Chakra:** Heart
- **Zodiac sign:** Leo
- **Best for:** Abundance, Confidence, Balance

Phantom Quartz – Has the ability to bring balance to your body. As a crown chakra crystal, it regulates the flow of energy from the root to the crown. Naturally brings harmony to the subtle energies in your aura. Stabilize the yin and yang, making you more aware of your partner's needs in a relationship and balancing both sides of your personality and character. Infuses you with a sense of pure love and joy by tapping into the Universe's unconditional love for you.

- **Chakra:** Crown
- **Zodiac sign:** All
- **Best for:** Balance, Stability, Love

Pink Quartz - Stone of the heart, known for its ability to dissolve emotional barriers that keep us from experiencing true love and intimacy. Emits lush feminine energy that envelops its wearer in feelings of self-love, self-acceptance, and self-worth, easing anxiety, stress, and tension. Those struggling with grief or heartbreak will find much comfort in Pink Quartz.

- **Chakra:** Heart
- **Zodiac sign:** Scorpio
- **Best for:** Unconditional Love, Self-Love, Healing Heartache, Comfort, Anxiety Relief, Stress Relief

Pink Sapphire – Tremendous strength. Like bamboo swaying with the wind instead of against it, Pink Sapphire is strong yet flexible. Bending rather than breaking in the face of adversity, this stone shows us how to face up to life's challenges with indomitable grace. Forgiveness, compassion, and unconditional love are all gifts of Pink Sapphire. Helps to let go of the past and move forward into the future with hope and optimism.

- **Chakra:** Heart
- **Zodiac sign:** Taurus
- **Best for:** Forgiveness, Compassion, Unconditional Love, Letting Go, Moving Forward

Pink Tourmaline - Relieving stress. Empowers you to interact on the physical plane from a higher spiritual perspective and holds the power to attract the divine will into your life. The loving energy of your higher self and of your Divine Counterpart are naturally in tune with Pink Tourmaline. Fills your emotional body with positive energy and provides all the emotional support that you need. Helps you find your way towards self-love, which is the root of all emotional wellbeing.

- **Chakra:** Heart
- **Zodiac sign:** Libra
- **Best for:** Spirituality, Positivity, Self-Love

Que Sera Stone - One of the most uplifting energetic tools ever discovered. If you want to pinpoint your true desire, Que Sera Stone will actively focus all of its powerful healing energy into understanding and revealing your desire. It urges you to create your own destiny.

- **Chakra:** All
- **Zodiac sign:** None
- **Best for:** Energy Healing, Positive Energy, Metaphysical Healing, Truth

Rhodonite - Deep love and compassion, forgiveness. It supports you in managing painful memories and moving on from unhealthy or abusive situations. Comfort. Bridges the gap between you and your loved ones, by instilling a sense of harmony and gentle communication styles.

- **Chakra:** Heart
- **Zodiac sign:** Taurus
- **Best for:** Compassion, Forgiveness, Harmony

Rose Quartz – The unconditional love crystal. It represents universal, agape love for oneself, the universe, all others, and all living things. Emanates femininity, openness, elevation, and deepening of love. Opens your heart to receiving love, giving love, and truly experiencing what it means to be joyful. Capable of restoring harmony where there is discord, even if that discord is found within oneself. In a relationship, it can help deepen eros love and build an elevated level of communication.

- **Chakra:** Heart
- **Zodiac sign:** Libra, Taurus
- **Best for:** Love, Joy, Harmony

Sapphire – Sapphire comes in many different hues. Blue Sapphire connects to water energy, bringing a deep sense of serenity and peace at all times, through obstacles and challenges. It also attunes your thoughts and ideas to divine wisdom and facilitates intellectual processes. Pink Sapphire increases deep emotional awareness and healing, and Yellow Sapphire connects you with the powers of the sun. It brings clarity to the direction of your life. Green Sapphire clears negative energies from your heart, and Star Sapphire sharpens your inner vision.

- **Chakra:** Third eye, heart, solar plexus
- **Zodiac sign:** Virgo
- **Best for:** Wisdom, Awareness, Vision

Selenite - Cleansing your environment and charging other crystals. It's a self-cleanser, which means it doesn't even need to be recharged. Selenite doesn't absorb negative energy, transforming it into healing rays of loving light. Mental clarity and boosting your intentions.

- **Chakra:** Crown
- **Zodiac sign:** Taurus
- **Best for:** Clarity, Cleansing, Intentions

Seraphinite – Helps with starting over and to look for happiness and joy. Repel negative energy while also promoting revival. It will provide brilliant opportunities for the new life you are attempting to build. Clears all blockages in your chakras, providing a pure aura. Brings peace of mind and inspire you to move forward in life with a sense of purpose.

- **Chakra:** Crown, Third eye, Throat, Heart, Solar Plexus, Sacral, Root.
- **Zodiac sign:** Sagittarius

- **Best for:** Opportunities, New beginnings, Inner peace, Passion, Inspiration.

Snowflake Obsidian – A purifying stone that can help you attain peace and serenity. Detoxifies the emotional body, declutters the mind from negative energy, and lets your emotions flow freely. Meditating with the Snowflake Obsidian stone will allow you to expand your consciousness and discover more about yourself. Known as the stone of purity, brings balance to your mind, body, and spirit. Empowers your soul and enables you to carve a space for yourself that is separate from the chaos of the world.

- **Chakra:** Root
- **Zodiac sign:** Capricorn, Virgo
- **Best for:** Purification, Discovery, Balance

Sodalite – Calming and empowering. Enhances communication, improves emotional wellbeing, and boosts mental clarity. It allows you to convey your emotional, spiritual, and mental processes and feelings with clarity and ease, helping you to be understood by people easier. Removes energy blockages from your spiritual body. Brings wisdom and insight from the Universe.

- **Chakra:** Third eye
- **Zodiac sign:** Pisces, Sagittarius
- **Best for:** Clarity, Communication, Wisdom

Strawberry Quartz – Deeply connected to the Universe's unconditional love, thus allowing deep and pure love to flow through your entire emotional body. It transcends the physical world to reach higher energies of love that are then poured into your life and washed over you, so that you can discover the true meaning that binds us all. Attain peace of mind through the beauty of love.

- **Chakra:** Heart

- **Zodiac sign:** Libra
- **Best for:** Love, Self-Discovery, Peace

Sunstone - Positive energy, brings good luck, and fortune to all of your endeavors. Cope better with the challenges and obstacles in your life, overcome them with motivation and drive. Instills a sense of zest for life in you. Sunstone is said to be a great teacher of self-worth and self-confidence. It encourages you to go after the things that light you up, so you can create the life you've always wanted.

- **Chakra:** Sacral
- **Zodiac sign:** Libra, Leo
- **Best for:** Positivity, Zest, Confidence

Tanzanite -Tanzanite is a stunning blue crystal variety of Zoisite. Connect your crown, third eye, and heart chakras, connects your heart, mind, and soul to bring out your true self. It increases capacity for compassion while also enhancing intellect. Exposes lies you tell yourself, assisting you in becoming more honest and truthful to yourself. You will be able to say more constructive things and let go of arguments and disagreements. It's akin to shedding old skin to accept your true self.

- **Chakra:** Etheric, Crown, Third eye, Throat, Heart
- **Zodiac sign:** Gemini
- **Best for:** Inter-dimensional Communication, Spiritual Awakening, Awareness, Truth, Sense of Purpose.

Tibetan Quartz – Aura cleanser, provides emotional, spiritual, and physical healing. Elevates people to a higher path that leads to pure spiritual connections. Courage to deal with unexpected changes and provide clarity and guidance. It is prevalent for increasing wealth and improving one's financial situation. It is a magnificent healer, it also aids in healing the nervous system, surgical aftereffects, and pain relief.

- **Chakra:** All Chakras
- **Zodiac sign:** All
- **Best for:** Cleansing Aura, Courage, Spiritual Connections, Peace, Healing.

Tiger's Eye – Activating the seat of personal power, determination, willpower, and self-belief. If there is a project that you're passionate about, Tiger's Eye will help you see it through to the bitter end. It promotes perseverance and encourages a can-do attitude. Protects from the negative intentions of others, and is said to shelter you from the gaze of the evil eye. The most common form of Tiger's Eye predominantly activates the solar plexus chakra, but other variants can open up different chakras.

- **Chakra:** Solar Plexus, Third Eye, Root, Throat
- **Zodiac sign:** Gemini
- **Best for:** Protection, Willpower, Self-Belief, Self-Esteem

Topaz - Heal, soothe, and stimulate both body and mind. Cleanse and balance energy levels to reveal the truth of your being. Positive vibrations, this stone helps to reduce stress and tension, making it that much easier for joy, good fortune, and abundance to enter your life. Though all Topaz stones share these basic properties, each type of topaz has unique colorations and energies. Blue Topaz, for instance, is perfect for tapping into your inner confidence and wisdom, while yellow topaz brings happiness, creativity, and good fortune.

- **Chakra:** Solar Plexus, Throat, Crown, Etheric, Root, Sacral
- **Zodiac sign:** Sagittarius, Scorpio, Leo
- **Best for:** Healing, Positivity, Emotional Balance, Self-Awareness

Tourmaline – Tourmaline comes in varying shades. Black Tourmaline is a grounding and centering stone that gives you a sense of certainty and confidence, while Pink Tourmaline cultivates a deep emotional connection between you and your loved ones. Purple Tourmaline enhances mental calmness and serenity, Green Tourmaline channels health, vitality, and life to every fiber of your being, so that you are infused with courage and strength. Blue Tourmaline supports you in dealing with challenges and obstacles in your life, bringing you peace and tranquility.

- **Chakra:** Root, heart, crown, third eye, throat
- **Zodiac sign:** Libra, Capricorn, Scorpio
- **Best for:** Grounding, Vitality, Strength

Tree Agate – Connects you to feng shui, allowing you to harmonize the energies of the Universe for the highest good. It also propels you in your personal development journeys, encouraging you to challenge ourselves and reach new heights. Brings a quiet energy that dispels negative energy and enhances inner stability. This encourages you to cope with life's challenges in a more harmonious and mature manner. Propels you towards spiritual growth.

- **Chakra:** Heart
- **Zodiac sign:** Virgo, Taurus, Gemini
- **Best for:** Personal Growth, Stability, Calmness

Turquoise – Supports the revitalization of all your chakras. Clears blockages and stagnant energy from your energy fields and replaces them with healing and soothing energy. Assists you in cultivating a more hopeful and optimistic outlook in life. Positive vibrations shield you from negativity in your surroundings and protect you from potential mishaps, harmonizing your energy and recharging your emotional body.

- **Chakra:** Throat
- **Zodiac sign:** Sagittarius
- **Best for:** Revitalization, Optimism, Positivity

Umbalite – Inner strength, calming influence, we can see the love and compassion that underlie all of our actions, both positive and negative. It helps us to forgive ourselves for our mistakes and to move forward with confidence in our gifts and abilities. Able to unlock the door to our innermost emotions, this stone can be an invaluable ally in the treatment of heart and lung disorders, as well as enhancing our sexuality and overall metabolism.

- **Chakra:** Heart, Root, Crown
- **Zodiac sign:** Aquarius
- **Best for:** Healing, Compassion, Forgiveness, Self-Worth, Emotional Balance

Vivianite – Healing stone for the physical body, specifically the teeth and bones. Prevents memory loss relating to dementia or trauma. A heart-healing crystal, for finding balance in the heart chakra. Come to terms with your emotions and translate them into conscious actions.

- **Chakra:** Heart, Throat, Third Eye, Crown
- **Zodiac sign:** Capricorn
- **Best for:** Balance, Heart-Healing, Compassion

White Sapphire – Peace and serenity, wisdom and gives you the strength of spirit to act. Communicating with the Higher Self and seeking spiritual guidance is made easier with White Sapphire, as it opens and activates the Crown Chakra. It breaks down your unconscious defenses and allows you to see the true beauty of this mortal world and your place in it, with fresh, childlike eyes.

- **Chakra:** Crown, Third Eye
- **Zodiac sign:** Taurus

- **Best for:** Wisdom, Strength, Spirituality, Insight, Guidance, Protection

Xanthite – Xanthite stones are rare crystals that belong in the Tourmaline family. Hard gemstones, they can be worn on jewelry and make for immense success talismans. These yellow-brown gems banish negative vibes from your aura and encourage you to pursue your dreams. They inspire determination, courage, and self-confidence.

- **Chakra:** Solar Plexus
- **Zodiac sign:** None
- **Best for:** Determination, Courage, Self-Confidence

Yellow Calcite - Increases memory and self-worth. Retention of key concepts and information. Builds self-confidence. Eliminator of accumulated self-doubt, overall enhancing energy levels. It allows you to tap into your own personal motivation and personal power. Powerful energy cleanser that you can use to regain balance and harmony in your energy fields.

- **Chakra:** Solar plexus
- **Zodiac sign:** Cancer, Leo, Pisces
- **Best for:** Memory, Self-Confidence, Willpower

Zircon - The oldest mineral on Earth, Associated with all seven chakras. Cleanse and purify your soul, removing any negativity that may be holding you back. Combat any evil forces or spirits by redirecting your surplus energies back to the earth, bringing you closer to the Divine, and awakening your own spiritual power. Connect with your higher self or achieve spiritual enlightenment. Zircon allows you to access previously hidden knowledge and understanding.

- **Chakra:** Root, Sacral, Solar-Plexus, Heart, Throat, Third-Eye, Crown
- **Zodiac sign:** Leo, Aries, Sagittarius
- **Best for:** Spiritual Guidance, Protection, Connection with Higher Self, Enlightenment

Seventeen

Oil's, & Aroma's

"I placed a bowl of herbs and ointments in the window of my bedroom, and let the scented breeze carry him away . . ."
– Sherry Jones

Aromatherapy has played an inherent role in spiritual and healing practices throughout history. This is because essential oils, aromatic herbs, and incense can be used to promote a sense of relaxation, and grounding, and even inspire a connection to spirit. Essential oils have a variety of uses including spells, potions, mediations and more.

Helpful Essential Oils

Frankincense - Frankincense is one of the most sacred essential oils for spirituality. It has been used in different spiritual rituals and ceremonies – for healing, cleansing and enlightenment – in many different cultures, for thousands of years. It helps to increase our faith and connection to our higher self.

Myrrh - Myrrh was used in ancient temple worship as an ingredient in the holy anointing oil for consecrating priests and kings. Myrrh has one of the highest levels of sesquiterpene in an essential oil. Sesquiterpene's deletes bad information in cellular memory so inhaling this oil can help to eliminate negative thoughts. It can help reduce stress, bring focus and can assist in a deep spiritual "opening" while bringing calm and tranquility.

Sandalwood - Sandalwood has been used for thousands of years to calm the mind and relieve anxiety, reduce signs of aging and skin inflammation. It has spiritual significance and is said to bring devotees closer to the divine. Sandalwood is helpful in healing emotional and spiritual wounds, as it opens the heart and helps to promote trust. It's also quite grounding.

Neroli - Neroli or orange blossom has a pleasant floral fragrance and can help you to be more self-accepting, face your fears and accept the work you need to do for yourself. The fragrance can also inspire creativity and encourage regular spiritual practice.

Rose - Rose is the fragrance of love, both the human and the Divine kind. It opens the heart to receive love, particularly self-love and a deeper connection to the spiritual world.

Vetiver - Vetiver is extremely grounding and can be especially beneficial if you tend to wander and lose focus during your meditation practice.

Palo Santo - Palo Santo is a cousin to Frankincense and loosely translated means Holy Wood. It has been used for hundreds of years by healers for spiritual applications. It is grounding and calming and can elicit a sense of peacefulness and calm.

Cedarwood – Cedarwood encourages us to focus inward. It can also help to illuminate your need for meditation and return you to your spiritual path when obstacles have made it difficult.

Lavender – Lavender is one of the most versatile oils. It is readily available and there are many different varieties. Lavender is known for its relaxation properties and helps promote sleep. It blends well with most other oils.

Bergamot – Bergamot has an underlying floral and citrus scent which has an emotional uplifting effect and is great for helping alleviate depressive, sad, or grief-stricken emotional states.

Ylang Ylang – Ylang Ylang is a deeply calming and sedative oil. It can help release feelings of anger, tension, and mixes well with patchouli and frankincense.

Sage – Sage is cleaning and purifying and can assist in removing negative energies. It is grounding and restores both balance and energy.

Peppermint – Peppermint is a popular oil for visualization that is said to stimulate the mind to help support memory, focus, concentration, and mental performance.

Sweet orange – Citrus oils like lemon and orange are very uplifting to the mind and body. Lemon, when used aromatically, promotes physical energy and purification.

Bergamot – Bergamot oil helps us in the areas of self-love, self-worth, self-acceptance, self-judgment, and self-loathing. This oil helps do the work necessary to step out of one's fears of not being good enough, and habits of holding back for fear of rejection.

Frankincense – In addition to alleviating depression and low mood, Frankincense is known as the "Oil of Truth", revealing deceptiveness and false truths. It invites the individual to let go of lower vibrations, insults, and negativity. This oil helps create new perspectives based on integrity and enlightenment.

Patchouli Essential Oil – When diffused, Patchouli can help alleviate nervous tension and worry and is a soothing oil for meditation. The aroma removes nervous exhaustion and restlessness while also increasing mental activity in preparation for conscious dreams.

Eighteen

Spells

Spells Basics:

1. Set a clear intention
2. Raise energy
3. Direct that energy towards your goal
4. Close the spell with gratitude

Simple Spell Examples:

1. Clarity Spell

- Gather a clear quartz crystal and a blue candle
- Light the candle, hold the crystal
- Visualize mental fog clearing, replaced by bright light
- Say: "Clarity come, confusion leave, clear thoughts I now receive"

2. Abundance Spell

- Collect three green leaves
- Place them in a circle around a coin
- Visualize prosperity flowing into your life
- Chant: "Leaves of green, bring wealth unseen"

3. Protection Spell

- Find a small stick and some black string
- Tie the string around the stick, focusing on safety
- Say: "With this knot, I bind protection tight, keep me safe both day and night"

Gathering Supplies in Nature:

1. Always ask permission before taking from nature
2. Take only what you need
3. Leave an offering (e.g., water, birdseed) in return
4. Collect responsibly, avoiding rare or protected species

Using Nature in Spells:

1. Trees for grounding and strength
2. Flowing water for cleansing and emotion
3. Stones for stability and specific energies
4. Flowers for love and beauty
5. Leaves for growth and change

Energy Work in Spells:

1. Center yourself through deep breathing
2. Visualize energy building within you
3. Direct this energy into your spell components
4. Release the energy with strong intention

The most important component in any spell is your focused intention and belief. These practices are meant to help you connect with nature and your own inner power.

Youth Potion: Ingredients:

- 1 cup spring water
- 3 fresh mint leaves
- 1 slice of lemon
- 1 small rose quartz crystal

Process:

1. Under a waxing moon, combine water, mint, and lemon in a glass jar
2. Place rose quartz in the jar
3. Set outside overnight to absorb moonlight
4. In the morning, strain and drink while visualizing youthful energy
5. Chant: "Youth and vitality, flow through me"

Aura Cleansing: Supplies:

- White sage or palo santo
- Feather (optional)

Process:

1. Light the sage or palo santo

2. Starting at your feet, move the smoke up your body
3. Use the feather or your hand to waft smoke around you
4. Visualize negative energy dissolving
5. Say: "Negativity depart, my aura shines clear and bright"

Drawing Success Spell: Supplies:

- Green candle
- Cinnamon stick
- Bay leaf
- Pen

Process:

1. Write your specific goal on the bay leaf
2. Light the green candle
3. Hold the cinnamon stick, focusing on your goal
4. Pass the bay leaf through the candle flame (carefully!)
5. Burn the bay leaf in a fireproof dish
6. Chant: "As this leaf turns to ash, my success comes in a flash"
7. Let the candle burn out safely

Remember, these practices are symbolic rituals meant to focus your intention and energy. The real power comes from within you. Always practice fire safety and be respectful when using natural materials.

Nineteen

Amulet's & Talisman's

"Love is the vital essence that pervades and permeates, from the center to the circumference, the graduating circles of all thought and action. Love is the talisman of human weal and woe-the open sesame to every soul."

- *Elizabeth Cady Stanton*

Amulets

Amulets provide protection from danger; and a **talisman** is used to attract a particular benefit to its owner.

Natural amulets are of many kinds: stones, crystals, gems, metals, teeth and claws of animals, bones, plants, and so on. Man-made amulets, equally varied, include religious medallions and small figurines.

"God did extraordinary miracles through Paul, so that even handkerchiefs and aprons that had touched him were taken to the sick, and their illnesses were cured and the evil spirits left them." Acts 19:11‑12

Most amulets are worn close to the heart or above the waste. When choosing yours, as always pray first, seek the Divine for wisdom. Listen to your inner Magick and your amulet will find you. Before wearing anything make sure you cleanse/charge the object. Consecrate and dedicate the amulets' purpose.

Talismans

An object, typically an <u>inscribed</u> ring or stone, that is thought to have magick powers and to bring good luck. [5]

---

[5] Definitions from <u>Oxford Languages</u>

Used and revered since the Stone Age, talismans are objects believed to be imbued with magickal properties, and are intended to guide, empower, and protect the owner from danger, evil, harm, and sickness.[6]

Something as simple as your lucky rabbit's foot could be your talisman. Just like an amulet, dedicate your chosen talisman's purpose. Cleanse and charge as often as you feel lead.

There are three common types of talismans. Talismans carried or wore on the body, talismans hung upon or above the bed of an infirm person, and medicinal talismans.

Twenty

Symbols

Symbols have played a significant role in spirituality across cultures and throughout history.

Historical Use of Symbols in Spirituality:

1. Ancient Egypt:
   - Ankh: symbol of life
   - Eye of Horus: protection and healing
2. Hinduism:
   - Om: the sound of the universe
   - Lotus: purity and enlightenment
3. Buddhism:
   - Dharma Wheel: the eightfold path
   - Buddha's footprint: presence of the Buddha
4. Christianity:
   - Cross: faith and salvation

- Fish: early Christian symbol
5. Celtic:
    - Triquetra: trinity or interconnectedness
    - Tree of Life: connection between heaven and earth
6. Native American:
    - Dreamcatcher: protection from bad dreams
    - Medicine Wheel: harmony and connections
7. Wicca/Neopaganism:
    - Pentagram: five elements
    - Triple Moon: maiden, mother, crone aspects

How Symbols Are Used:

1. Meditation focus
2. Protective talismans
3. Ritual tools
4. Sacred geometry in architecture
5. Body art or jewelry
6. Visualization aids

Creating a Personal Power Symbol

1. Reflect on your spiritual goals and values
2. Sketch ideas combining meaningful shapes/images
3. Refine your design to a simple, reproducible form
4. Charge your symbol through meditation or ritual

Practical Exercise: Let's create a symbol for inner strength and use it in a simple practice.

1. Design your symbol:
   - Draw a circle (wholeness)
   - Add a vertical line through it (strength)
   - Place a small triangle at the top (direction, aspiration)
2. Charging ritual:
   - Draw the symbol on paper with a blue pen (blue for communication and truth)
   - Hold the paper in your hands
   - Close your eyes and visualize the symbol glowing with energy

- o Chant or speak your intention: "This symbol represents my inner strength"
  - o Repeat for several minutes, feeling the energy build
3. Using the symbol:
  - o Carry the paper with you
  - o Visualize the symbol when you need strength
  - o Draw it on your skin with a skin-safe pen before challenging situations
  - o Incorporate it into meditation by visualizing it at your solar plexus chakra

Remember, the power of symbols comes from the meaning and energy you invest in them. This practice can help focus your intention and serve as a tangible reminder of your inner resources.

Twenty-One

Spirit animals, Mediums, & Pets

Spirit animals, mediums, and pets in spirituality, along with practical applications:

Spirit Animals:

- Concept originates from various indigenous cultures
- Believed to be guides, protectors, or embodiments of qualities
- Can be lifelong companions or appear for specific situations

Practical Application:

1. Identify your spirit animal:
   - Meditate on the question "What is my spirit animal?"
   - Pay attention to recurring animal encounters in life or dreams

- o   Take note of animals you've always felt drawn to

2. Connect with your spirit animal:
   - o   Research its characteristics and symbolism
   - o   Meditate while visualizing the animal
   - o   Create or obtain an image or figurine of the animal as a focus object

3. Seek guidance:
   - o   Before making decisions, visualize your spirit animal and ask for insight
   - o   Observe the animal's behavior in nature for lessons

Mediums:

- Individuals believed to communicate with spirits or the deceased
- Practiced in various forms across cultures and throughout history
- Often use different methods: clairvoyance, clairaudience, clairsentience

Practical Application:

1. Develop your own intuitive abilities:
   - Practice meditation to quiet your mind
   - Keep a dream journal to enhance your subconscious awareness
   - Try automatic writing: relax, hold a pen, and let your hand move freely
2. Create a communication space:
   - Designate a quiet area in your home
   - Use calming elements like candles or incense
   - Display photos of loved ones who have passed
3. Simple communication exercise:
   - Sit quietly in your space
   - Focus on a specific person or question
   - Pay attention to any thoughts, feelings, or images that arise
   - Record your experiences in a journal

Pets in Spirituality:

- Many cultures view animals as spiritual beings
- Pets often considered family members with spiritual significance
- Some believe pets can be spiritual protectors or guides

Practical Application:

1. Mindful interaction:
    - Practice being fully present when with your pet
    - Observe their behavior for lessons in living in the moment
2. Energy work with pets:
    - Try gentle pet massage, focusing on sending loving energy
    - Practice meditation with your pet nearby, visualizing a connection between your energies
3. Pet blessing ritual:

- Create a simple altar with pet-safe plants and a bowl of fresh water
- Light a candle (safely away from your pet)
- Hold or sit with your pet
- Speak words of blessing and protection for your pet

4. Intuitive communication:
- Sit quietly with your pet
- Mentally ask them a question
- Pay attention to any impressions, feelings, or images that come to you
- Practice regularly to develop your connection

Twenty-Two

Vibrations, & the Law of Attraction

Vibrations:

- Based on the idea that everything in the universe is energy vibrating at different frequencies
- Higher vibrations are associated with positive emotions and experiences
- Lower vibrations are linked to negative states

Law of Attraction:

- Principle suggesting that we attract experiences that match our dominant thoughts and feelings
- Based on the idea that like attracts like in the energetic realm

Practical Applications:

1. Raise Your Vibration:
    - Practice gratitude: Daily list 3-5 things you're thankful for
    - Use positive affirmations: "I am worthy of love and success"
    - Engage in activities you enjoy: music, art, nature walks
    - Exercise and maintain a healthy diet
    - Meditate or practice mindfulness regularly
2. Visualize Your Desires:
    - Create a vision board with images of your goals
    - Spend 5-10 minutes daily visualizing your ideal life in detail
    - Engage all senses in your visualization
3. Align Thoughts and Feelings:
    - Monitor your self-talk, replacing negative thoughts with positive ones

- o Practice feeling the emotions of already having what you want
  - o Use the "as if" technique: Act as if you already have your desire
4. Energy Cleansing:
   - o Smudge your space with sage or palo santo
   - o Take salt baths to clear your energy field
   - o Use crystals like clear quartz or black tourmaline for energy purification
5. Manifestation Ritual:
   - o Write your desire on paper
   - o Hold the paper while focusing on the feeling of achievement
   - o Burn the paper safely, releasing your desire to the universe
6. Vibration-Raising Meditation:
   - o Sit comfortably and close your eyes
   - o Visualize a warm, golden light entering through your crown

- o Imagine this light filling your body, raising your vibration
- o Repeat a high-vibration word like "love" or "joy"

7. Frequency Matching:
   - o Identify the "frequency" of your goal (e.g., abundance, love)
   - o Surround yourself with things that match this frequency
   - o For abundance: Carry a prosperity crystal, use green in your environment

8. Scripting:
   - o Write a detailed description of your ideal day as if it's already happening
   - o Include sensory details and emotions
   - o Read it daily to align your energy with this reality

9. The 5x55 Method:
   - o Choose an affirmation aligned with your goal
   - o Write it 55 times a day for 5 consecutive days

- o Focus on the feeling of achievement as you write

10. Letting Go:
    - o After setting your intention, practice detachment
    - o Trust the process and avoid obsessing over outcomes
    - o Focus on feeling good in the present moment

Twenty-Three

Using Creative Visual's, and Thought to manifest

- Based on the idea that our thoughts and visual imagination can influence reality
- Rooted in various spiritual and psychological traditions
- Combines elements of visualization, focused intention, and belief

Practical Applications:

1. Vision Boarding:
   - Gather magazines, photos, and inspirational quotes
   - Create a collage representing your goals and desires
   - Place it where you'll see it daily
   - Spend a few minutes each day focusing on the board, feeling the emotions of

achievement

2. Mental Movies:
    - o Close your eyes and visualize your goal as a detailed movie
    - o Include all senses: sights, sounds, smells, textures
    - o Practice this for 5-10 minutes daily, preferably right before sleep

3. Treasure Mapping:
    - o Draw a map of your ideal life
    - o Include symbols or images representing your goals
    - o Add a legend explaining each symbol
    - o Review and update regularly

4. Manifestation Box:
    - o Decorate a small box
    - o Write your desires on slips of paper
    - o Place them in the box with small objects representing your goals
    - o Hold the box daily, focusing on your intentions

5. Dream Journaling:
   - Keep a journal by your bed
   - Record dreams immediately upon waking
   - Look for symbols or messages related to your goals
   - Use these insights to refine your visualization practice

6. Guided Imagery:
   - Record yourself describing your ideal scenario
   - Listen to this recording regularly, fully immersing yourself in the experience

7. Mind Movies:
   - Create a digital slideshow of images representing your goals
   - Add inspiring music and affirmations
   - Watch it daily, engaging your emotions

8. Visualization Meditation:
   - Start with a relaxation exercise

- Visualize yourself in your ideal scenario
- Engage all senses and feel the positive emotions
- Practice for 10-15 minutes daily

9. Future Self Journaling:
   - Write entries from the perspective of your future self who has achieved the goals
   - Be detailed about how life looks, feels, and what you've accomplished
   - Read these entries regularly to reinforce the vision

10. Affirmation Artwork:
    - Create art (drawing, painting, digital) that incorporates your affirmations
    - Use colors and symbols that resonate with your goals
    - Display the artwork prominently

11. Manifestation Altar:

Designate a small space for your
manifestation focus

Include objects, images, and words
representing your desires

Spend time daily at this altar, visualizing
and feeling your goals

12. Scripting:
    o Write a detailed story of your
      ideal life as if it's happening
      now
    o Include sensory details and
      emotions
    o Read this script daily, fully
      immersing yourself in the
      story

Remember, the key to these
practices is consistency and engagement.

The goal is to make your desires
feel real and attainable in your mind.

Combine these visualization
techniques with positive action steps
towards your goals for best results.

Phoenix Tree Gallery ™ ®